GHOSTS OF
VIRGINIA'S
TIDEWATER

Believe!

L B Taylor

GHOSTS OF VIRGINIA'S TIDEWATER

L.B. TAYLOR JR.

Haunted
America

Published by Haunted America A Division of
The History Press
Charleston, SC 29403
www.historypress.net

Cover images: Front cover of lighthouse at Old Point Comfort on Fort Monroe, photo by
Michael Westfall. Back cover photos by author.

First published 2011

Manufactured in the United States

ISBN 978.1.60949.226.7

Library of Congress Cataloging-in-Publication Data

Taylor, L. B.
Ghosts of Virginia's Tidewater / L.B. Taylor, Jr.
p. cm.
Includes bibliographical references.
ISBN 978-1-60949-226-7
1. Ghosts--Virginia--Tidewater Region. 2. Haunted places--Virginia--Tidewater Region.
I. Title.
BF1472.U6T387 2011
133.109755'1--dc22
2011009163

CONTENTS

CONTENTS

INTRODUCTION

Ask Virginians what the Tidewater section of the state is, and most will say that it is the southeastern area running from Chesapeake, Portsmouth and Virginia Beach on the south end to Gloucester and Mathews Counties northward, moving west through Hampton, Newport News and Williamsburg, halfway to Richmond. Technically, however, the name "Tidewater" may correctly be applied to all portions of the commonwealth where the water level is affected by the tides.

When it comes to metaphysical activity, Tidewater Virginia ranks as one of the richest in the country. Edgar Cayce, arguably the greatest American psychic, believed that because two large bodies of water (the Chesapeake Bay and the Atlantic Ocean) were involved, the area was particularly conducive to paranormal forces. Add to this the fact that in Virginia's more than four hundred years of civilized settlement, there has been more trauma and tragedy here than in any other state in the union—elements, experts contend, that create fertile spawning grounds for spectral phenomena.

The hauntings here date from the earliest days of Jamestown in the seventeenth century to the present and range from "traditional" ghosts to overactive poltergeists and unexplained mysteries that have withstood the test of time. Tidewater is a land laden with legends and lore, all part of its unmatched cultural heritage. Enjoy!

PART I

NORTHERN AREA

TRAGIC TEARDROPS IN THE SNOW

Church Hill is a large frame house that stands on an elevation just above the Ware River in Gloucester. It is here where one of Virginia's most tragic stories occurred. In the 1700s, when the Throckmorton family owned the place, they had a beautiful young daughter, Elizabeth. Her father once took her to London, where she met a handsome English gentleman with whom she fell deeply in love. The couple vowed eternal faithfulness to each other and arranged to complete plans for their wedding by correspondence. Elizabeth's father, however, was staunchly against the match and intercepted the letters so that neither ever again heard from the other after Elizabeth returned to Gloucester.

In time, as Elizabeth longed for her lost love, she fell ill and apparently died. Friends contended that she had lost the will to live and pined away. On a blustery November afternoon, near sunset, they buried her in the family graveyard at the foot of the garden.

According to longstanding legend, an evil butler, angered by some slight accorded him by the family, dug up the grave site that night and opened the coffin to steal valuable jewelry that had been buried with Elizabeth. One particular ring would not slip off her stiffened finger, so in his haste the servant severed the finger. To his horror, he suddenly found that the girl was not dead. She had lapsed into a deep cataleptic coma and had been presumed dead. The shock of having her finger cut off roused her. The terrified butler ran off into the night and was never heard from again.

Somehow, the frail girl, barefoot and thinly dressed, managed to climb out of the grave, crawl past the last dead stalks of the garden and drag herself through a driving snowstorm to the front of the house. There, in a weakened condition, she scratched feebly at the door. If her father, sitting inside before a roaring fire, heard her, he dismissed it as one of the dogs trying to come in out of the storm. Lost in his grief, he ignored the sound.

The next morning, Elizabeth's body was found at the doorstep beneath a blanket of snow. She had frozen to death. There was a trail of bloody footprints leading from the garden.

For years afterward, succeeding generations of Throckmortons swore that the spirit of Elizabeth remained in the house. Whenever the first snow fell each year, there would be sounds of a rustling skirt ascending the staircase, followed by the distinct sounds of the placing of logs in fireplaces and the crackling of a hearty fire in various rooms. Investigations would find no such logs and no fires. There also would be traces of blood in the snow following

Church Hill in Gloucester County is the site where the spirit of a young girl, who froze to death on the front doorstep, returns each winter to stoke the flames in fireplaces.

the route that Elizabeth had taken from the graveyard to the house. Such sounds and sights were experienced not once but rather many times and were attested to by various members of the family and their servants.

On one noteworthy occasion, generations later in 1879, Professor Warner Taliaferro, then head of the house, left home one evening to spend the night at a friend's house. Neighbors reported that in the midst of a fierce storm they saw Church Hill ablaze with lights. Junius Brown, passing by on horseback, rode up to the house to see if his sisters, visiting in the neighborhood, had sought shelter from the storm there. There was no one home. Servants, living in their quarters on the property, also saw the lights and assumed that Mr. Taliaferro had returned. He had not. The mystery was never explained.

The most telling psychic phenomenon, though, concerns the violets that grow in lush profusion near the steps to Church Hill. They are finer and more beautiful here than those in any other section of the grounds. It is said that they are watered by the tears of a dying girl seeking refuge from the season's first snow.

The Psychic Wonders of White Marsh

You have probably seen White Marsh in the movies and not realized it. This magnificent white-portico mansion, described as the epitome of southern plantations and known as the "Queen of Tidewater," has, in fact, been the exterior setting for a number of major films over the years. Situated strategically back from the Ware River in Gloucester, White Marsh stands amid a grant of land originally made in the 1640s. The Georgian Colonial house itself was built about a century later.

At one time, the estate included more than three thousand acres and was worked by 300 to 500 slaves. There are 1,500 slaves buried in a graveyard near the peach orchard. This vast expanse included forests, farmland, manicured lawns and gardens and rich fruit orchards, plus excellent crops of corn and soybeans. Eventually, the land passed to Evelina Matilda Prosser, who married John Tabb. After adding his wife's fortune to his own, Tabb was said to have been the richest man in Gloucester. Evelina has been described as a woman of great dignity, often gowned in black moiré antique.

Despite all of this splendor, however, Mrs. Tabb was not happy with the bucolic life. She had lost two of her children in infancy and wanted to move

The perfect setting for an antebellum movie scene, White Marsh in Gloucester County is allegedly haunted by the wife of a former owner whose pride was a paranormal rosebush.

to Norfolk or Williamsburg to enjoy a gayer social life. Mr. Tabb did not want to move, and he told his wife that if she would make herself content and remain in the country, he would create the finest garden in Virginia for her. It was then that the splendid terraced gardens were built, and many rare trees were planted in the park. The house also was remodeled, and wings and a pillared portico were added.

While Evelina, also affectionately known as "Mother Tabb," was pleased, there are indications that she was never totally happy at White Marsh. The deaths of her two infant children sent her into long periods of mourning. It was shortly after she and John died that the strange "occurrences" began. Phillip Tabb inherited the plantation from his parents, and as he lived in Baltimore, he placed it under the care of James Sinclair, returning only occasionally, with guests, during the fox hunting season.

Late one evening, Sinclair, returning to the house from town on horseback, was astonished to find every window ablaze with light. Fearing that his boss had come back without notice, he stabled his horse and rushed up the steps. The house was now dark and no one was inside. Curiously, the next year, the same thing happened to a caretaker named Franklin Dabney. He, too, approached White Marsh after being away one night, and he not only found every window lit but also clearly heard music and the sound of dancing. A bachelor, he bounded up the porch steps to participate in the merrymaking, but when he opened the door, there was only darkness and silence.

Years later, Reverend William Byrd Lee, then rector emeritus of Ware Church, and his wife paid a call to the mansion and were greeted by Catherine Tabb, granddaughter of Evelina. As they prepared to leave, the reverend went to bring his buggy to the door, and Mrs. Lee was seated alone in the hall. She happened to glance up the staircase, and her heart froze. She saw an elderly lady of stately and distinguished appearance descending the stairs. She was dressed in an old-fashioned costume of black moiré antique! The woman crossed the hall and disappeared into the dining room. It was then that Mrs. Lee suddenly realized that the figure was "not that of a mortal."

She called to her hostess and excitedly told her what she had witnessed. To her surprise, Catherine Tabb laughed and then explained that it was just Mother Tabb, who was often seen by members of the family. They also reported occasionally seeing Evelina enter a certain bedroom, open the lowest drawer of a bureau and remove all of the infant clothes inside it. Ever so carefully, she would take each article, shake it, refold it, place it back in the bureau and then slip quietly out of the room.

The Psychic Rosebush

Finally, there was the resistant rosebush. This occurred some years later, after the home had passed from the Tabbs to Mr. and Mrs. Hughes from New York. The pride of the garden was the proliferation of magnificent rosebushes. One May, they were full of buds, and on the second terrace was an especially luxuriant bush on which Mrs. Hughes found a full-blown rose with rich, creamy petals.

As she reached out to pick it, a most extraordinary thing happened. The bush began swaying violently, as if whipped by a strong wind. Mrs. Hughes looked around in dismay. There was not a breeze stirring. She tried again and again, but the bush trembled as if being shaken by unseen hands. Perturbed, she grabbed the stem firmly, but the bush was snatched from her hand and began swaying again. At that moment, the shutters of the house commenced banging sharply.

She fled to the house in terror and told her husband about it. He confidently approached the bush, but the same thing happened. A prudent man, he left it alone, fearing that if he did pluck the rose something disagreeable might happen. In time, the story of the incident spread throughout the county, and many visitors came to see the reluctant bush. Servants contended that it was the hand of Mother Tabb that had intervened. They said that it had been her favorite rose and that she allowed no one to snip it. Mrs. Hughes eventually grew nervous over the phenomenon, coupled with the banging of the shutters, and she ordered that the bush be destroyed.

Soon after, as she was making her rounds of the garden one morning, she found the rosebush gone, roots and all. She asked the gardener if he had dug it up as she had commanded. He told her, "No!"

THE RESPLENDENT RUINS OF ROSEWELL

Today, nearly three centuries after its construction began just off the northern shore of the York River in Gloucester County, the name Rosewell still evokes excitement, even though it has stood in ruins since being gutted in a 1916 fire. The accolades of this once magnificent mansion continue to ring true. Says Claude Lanciano, author of *Rosewell, Garland of Virginia*: "This masterpiece at the height of its glory in the mid-eighteenth century knew few rivals and has been called the finest example of colonial architecture in the country." Possibly the finest tribute was paid by noted American artist and author James Reynolds, who said, "I regard Rosewell as the finest house in Palladian style I have ever seen. I would rather own it, ruinous as it stands, than any other in the United States."

Construction on this palatial brick masterpiece began in 1725 under its landowner, Mann Page. It stood four stories high, with white marble casements and two turrets on the roof, inside of which were little rooms. The interior had five rooms on the first floor and a huge apartment used as a ballroom on the second. In all, the house consisted of thirty-five rooms, three wide halls and nine passageways. It was full of beautifully carved staircases, mantels and paneling that was said to have been exquisite beyond description.

Unfortunately, Mann Page never lived to see his great house finished. His son, Mann Page II, completed it in 1744. A generation later, Thomas Jefferson spent a great deal of time at Rosewell as the guest of his friend, John Page. Some historians believe that Jefferson may have penned a draft of the Declaration of Independence here.

The ruins of Rosewell in Gloucester County, once one of the most majestic manor homes in Virginia, have been the scene of a number of disturbing psychic encounters.

In its time, Rosewell was known throughout Virginia and the East Coast for its lavish parties and balls, attended by aristocratic gentlemen and hoop-skirted, velvet-dressed southern belles. Casks of the finest French wines and magnums of champagne were brought in by boat to wash down gourmet meals fit for a king. Scores of garlands of flowers, especially roses, richly decorated every room, and dances lasted until dawn. It was a grand time.

But Rosewell has its dark side, too. Many Gloucester natives have told stories of strange sightings and noises emanating from the rose-red brick foundation ruins. Some claim to have seen young servant boys standing beside the great pediment doorway at night, lighting the way for arriving phantom guests, who vanish ascending the Corinthian pilaster stairwell. Others swear that they hear violin and harpsichord music rising above the towering, still-standing chimneys.

Ronnie Miles, a native of neighboring Mathews County, had two scary psychic experiences at Rosewell about forty years ago. Once, he and a friend were exploring the ruins at night when they stumbled onto what may have been an old entrance to a wine cellar. Miles's friend lit a match to see better, only to have a flung brick knock the match out of his hand.

"I have to admit, it frightened the hell out of us," Miles said. "We had always heard a slave had been buried in the walls."

On the second occasion, Miles, another friend and two girls were all walking through the old Rosewell cemetery at night. He and his friend saw what appeared to be a light coming from the house ruins. Not wanting to scare the girls, they walked back to the site alone to investigate. "As we reached the perimeter of the ruins," Miles recalls, "we both were overcome by the most all-powerful stench I have ever smelled. It was potent. It literally drove us away."

Another chilling encounter was experienced by John Gulbranson—an amateur psychic investigator—his sister and some friends. One night about thirty years ago, they decided to go to the ruins. They drove down to the edge of two cornfields near the entrance road and got out there because the road had been blocked with a chain to discourage visitors. They had two guard dogs with them, but the dogs immediately began howling wildly and refused to budge. Previously, the dogs had never exhibited fear.

The dogs were tied to a tree, and the group walked through the cornfields and down the entrance road. A couple of the young men swore that they heard the sounds of a drummer coming from the Rosewell site, but when they got there they found nothing. They then retraced their steps back to the car. Just as they did, the dogs began barking furiously at the back window, and the hair on the dogs' backs stiffened. John and the others looked out the window, and a few yards away they all saw an African American man— suspended four or five feet above the ground! John's sister, Carol, began screaming hysterically, and they drove off, spinning the tires in the dirt. They had the distinct feeling that the man, or whatever it was, was following them, so they sped up.

A mile or so down the road, they stopped, got out and looked back. The man was gone. There was one small tree, only about an inch in diameter, at the side of the road, and it leaned out over the lane. Without warning, the tree began shaking violently, but there was no breeze, and they could see no cause for it. Terrified, they jumped back into the car and raced away. This time they didn't stop until they got back to civilization, and they pulled up under a streetlight. They got out and walked around the car. It was covered with dew. One of the group called the others to the rear of the car. There, in the dew, were the crystal-clear impressions of a baby's hand and a man's hand with a missing index finger.

Perhaps the scariest phenomenon of all at Rosewell was experienced by Raymond West, a local maintenance worker. He and a friend were joy riding

A scary scene: the skeletal remains of Rosewell.

with two young ladies when they decided to visit the ruins. It was about two o'clock in the morning, and the story is best told in West's own words:

There was an old dirt road that ran for about half a mile leading up to the place. As we made the last turn, there before us was an old black car with 1930s license plates blocking the driveway. It had old half-moon windows in the back and was facing away from us. It stunned us. I slammed on the brakes. You could see the car real well in the headlight beams. It was eerie.

Then, as we sat there in silence, we saw the head of a woman rise up in the rear window, and she stared at us. She had coal-black hair and a deathly ashen white face. We panicked. I tried to get the car in reverse, but the gears kept sticking, and all the time that woman kept looking at us, unblinking. Finally, I got the car in gear, and we burned rubber getting out of there. We pulled back a few hundred yards and then stopped. We were pretty shook up, but we decided to wait until daylight and check things out. There was no other way out of there, no other roads, paths or anything. If that car left, it had to go right past us.

At daybreak, we drove back down the driveway to the spot where we had seen it, and there was nothing there! The car and the woman had flatly disappeared. There were no tracks or anything. We looked everywhere but could find nothing. I tell you, I never believed in ghosts or anything like that, but to this day I can't explain what we saw or why.

All these and other mysterious manifestations possibly help explain why the artist-author James Reynolds once wrote: "Certainly, tremendous doings took place within the fire-riven walls of Rosewell. And what stories one hears of hauntings! All I hear seems in keeping with the magnificence and stature of this barren, deserted house."

THE MULTIPLE MYSTERIES OF OLD HOUSE WOODS

Of all the ghostly legends of Tidewater Virginia, perhaps none is more widely known—or has been told, retold, written and rewritten more often— than that of Old House Woods, also called Old Haunted Woods, located near the tiny crossroads town of Diggs in Mathews County, northeast of Gloucester. The colorful stories that have been passed down from generation to generation for more than two hundred years about this fifty-acre patch of pine woods and marshlands near the Chesapeake Bay contain some of the most bizarre and unusual psychic phenomena ever recorded.

Consider, for example, swashbuckling pirates burying stolen gold; retreating British soldiers hiding colonial treasure during the Revolutionary War; a full-rigged Spanish galleon that vanishes in thin air; skeletons in knights' armor wielding threatening swords; mysterious groups of shovelers digging furiously late at night; and ghost horses and cows that appear and disappear before one's eyes.

"Yes, it's true. All those tales and more have come out of Old House Woods," says Olivia Davis, a lifelong resident of the area. She should know. Her great-great-grandfather, James Forrest, bought this land in 1838, and it was kept in the family and farmed for more than a century. Old House Woods got its name, simply enough, from a large frame house that had a wood-covered plaster chimney and stood in the midst of the surrounding forest in the late 1700s. Later, after being abandoned for years, it fell into disrepair and thereafter became known as the "Old House."

"In the days before television, computers and even radio, telling stories was a popular pastime here," Olivia says. "Old-timers used to gather in the woods on Sundays and swap yarns. I can well remember my grandfather, Silas Forrest, talking about ghosts, and it was spellbinding." There are scores of others, residents and visitors alike, who also swear by them. And then there are those who have personally experienced the phenomena in one form or another. There is no way they will ever be shaken from their beliefs.

There are, allegedly, three reasons why Old House Woods are haunted. According to one legend, the crew of a pirate ship came ashore here in the seventeenth century, buried their treasure somewhere deep in the woods and then returned to sea, where they perished in a furious storm. That explains, say proponents of this theory, why mysterious figures have been seen digging in the woods on dark nights by the lights of tin lanterns. They are the pirate ghosts returning to claim their loot. In 1973, *Richmond Times-Dispatch* staff member Bill McKelway wrote, "Some say Blackbeard, the infamous Edward Teach, intercepted the treasure and then murdered the men who were hiding it."

A second possible reason may also have occurred in the second half of the seventeenth century. After being defeated at the Battle of Worcester in 1651, Charles II of England was said to have considered coming to Virginia. In preparation for his trip, a group of followers dispatched several chests of money, plate and jewels to the colony by ship. However, for some unexplained reason, the riches never reached Jamestown. Instead, the ship sailed up the Chesapeake Bay and anchored in waters at the mouth of White's Creek near Old House Woods. There, the treasure was offloaded, but before it could be safely hidden, the Royalists were attacked and murdered by a gang of indentured servants. In their rush to escape, these bondsmen took only part of the spoils, planning to come back later for the rest. But they, too, ran afoul of the elements. A sudden storm struck the bay, and all hands on board drowned when their ship capsized.

It may well be that the storms that took the lives of both the pirates and the renegades account for one of the many Old House Woods ghost traditions—that of the "Storm Woman." She has been described by those who claim to have seen her as "a wraith of a woman in a long nightgown, her long, fair hair flung back from her shoulders." Reportedly, whenever black clouds gather over this section of the bay, foretelling a coming gale, her figure rises above the tops of towering pine trees, and she wails loudly to warn watermen to take cover.

A third theory about the hauntings concerns an event that supposedly happened in late 1781, just before Lord Cornwallis's army was defeated by George Washington at Yorktown. The legend is that two British officers and four soldiers were entrusted with a huge amount of money. They slipped through enemy lines and headed north, hoping to find a British ship on the Chesapeake Bay. They managed to bury their riches in Old House Woods before they were found and killed by a unit of American cavalry. Thus, it may be their spirits that still hover over the site in eternal guard.

Whether one subscribes to one or more of these theories, or to none at all, they do offer some possible thoughts into why certain sights have appeared to a host of people in the area over the years. And the sightings have been prolific and explicit, however far-fetched they may sound today. One of the most celebrated incidents is attributed to Jesse Hudgins, described as a respectable merchant of unquestioned integrity, who ran a store in the town of Mathews Court House in the 1920s. Hudgins told of his experiences to a *Baltimore Sun* newspaper reporter in 1926, and he swore to its authenticity:

> *I do not care whether I am believed or not. I am not apologetic or ashamed to say I have seen ghosts in Old House Woods. I have seen them not once but a dozen times. I was 17 when I first actually saw a ghost. One October night I sat by the lamp reading. A neighbor whose child was very ill came asking me to drive to Mathews for a doctor. We had no telephone*

in those days. I hitched up and started to town. The night was gusty, clouds drifting over the moon, but I could see perfectly.

Nearing Old House Woods itself, I saw a light about 50 yards ahead moving along the road in the direction I was going. My horse, usually afraid of nothing, cowered and trembled violently. I felt rather uneasy myself. I have seen lights on the road at night, shining lanterns carried by men, but this light was different. There was something unearthly about it. The rays seemed to come from nowhere, and yet they moved with the bearer…

I gained on the traveler, and as I stand here before you, what I saw was a big man wearing a suit of armor. Over his shoulder was a gun, the muzzle end of which looked like a fish horn. As he strode, or floated along, he made no noise. My horse stopped still. I was weak with terror. I wasn't 20 feet from the thing, whatever it was, when it, too, stopped and faced me. At the same time, the woods about 100 feet from the wayfarer became alive with lights and moving forms. Some carried guns like the one borne by the man or thing in the road; others carried shovels of an outlandish type; while still others dug feverishly near a dead pine tree.

As my gaze returned to the first shadowy figure, what I saw was not a man in armor, but a skeleton, and every bone of it was visible through the iron of the armor, as though it were made of glass. The skull, which seemed to be illuminated from within, grinned at me horribly. Then, raising aloft a sword, which I had not hitherto noticed, the awful specter started towards me menacingly.

I could stand no more. Reason left me. When I came to it was broad daylight and I lay upon my bed at home. Members of my family said the horse had run away. They found me at the turn of the road beyond Old House Woods. We could not lead Tom [the horse] *by these woods for months afterwards.*

Hudgins's story, strange as it may seem, was corroborated some years later, according to newspaper accounts. One report noted:

A Richmond youth had tire trouble at a lonely spot along the road near the haunted woods one night very late. As he knelt in the road, a voice behind him asked, "Is this the king's highway? I have lost my ship." When the youth turned to look, he beheld a skeleton in armor within a few paces of him. Yelling like a maniac, the frightened motorist ran from the spot in terror and did not return for his car until the next day.

Perhaps the most unusual phenomenon sighted in Old House Woods is the legendary ghost ship. It allegedly has been seen by many. One of the most vivid accounts was given more than eighty years ago by Ben Ferbee, a fisherman who lived along the bay shore early in the twentieth century:

One starry night I was fishing off the mouth of White's Creek, well out in the bay. As the flood tide would not set in for some time, I decided to get the good fishing and come home with the early moon. It must have been after midnight when, as I turned to bait up a line in the stern of my boat, I saw a full-rigged ship in the bay, standing pretty well in. I was quite surprised, I tell you. Full-rigged ships were mighty scarce then. Besides that, I knew I was in for it if she kept that course. On the ship came, with lights at every masthead and spar. I was plumb scared.

They'll run me down and sink me, I thought. I shouted to sailors leaning over the rails forward, but they paid no heed to me. Just as I thought she would strike me, the helmsman put her hard aport and she passed so close that I was almost swamped by the wash. She was a beautiful ship, but different from any I had ever seen. She made no noise at all, and when she had gone by, the most beautiful harp and organ music I ever heard came back to me.

The ship sailed right up to the beach and never stopped, but kept right on. Over the sandy beach she swept, floating through the air and up to the Bay Shore road, her keel about twenty feet from the ground. I was scared out of my wits. I knew it was not a real ship. It was a ghost ship! Well, sir, I pulled up my anchor and started for home up White's Creek. I could see that ship hanging over Old House Woods, just as though she was anchored in the sea. And running down to the woods was a rope ladder, lined with the forms of men carrying tools and other contraptions.

When I got home my wife was up but had no supper for me. Instead, she and the children were praying. I knew what was the matter. Without speaking a word, she pointed to Old House Woods, a scared look on her face. She and the children had seen the ship standing over the woods. I didn't need to ask her. I started praying, too.

Soon after, Ferbee and his family moved from the area.

Many others claim to have sighted the fabled ghost ship. One was a fourteen-year-old Mathews County boy. "There was a big sailing ship floating in the marsh," he recalls. "It had two or three masts and was made of wood. There is only a foot of water there, but it looked like it was floating.

It was the kind of ship the pirates used. We watched it for about 100 yards more and then it just disappeared. I went home and told my mother, but she just laughed. She said everyone knew of the stories about the ghosts here."

Another who saw the phantom galleon, and many other things, too, was Harry Forrest, a farmer-fisherman who lived only six hundred yards from the edge of the woods. "I've seen more strange things in there than I could relate in a whole day," he once said before his death in the 1950s.

> I've seen armies of marching British redcoats. I've seen the "Storm Woman" and heard her dismal wailings, and my mother and I have sat here all hours of the night and seen lights in the woods. We have seen ships anchor off the beach and boats put into shore, and forms of men go to the woods. I would see lights over there and hear the sound of digging.
>
> I was out fishing right off the beach one day in broad daylight when I saw a full-rigged ship headed straight for me just 100 yards away. I rowed to shore as fast as I could, and just as I got on the beach, she started drifting, and she lifted and sailed straight to Old House Woods, and you heard the anchor chain clank.

There is a site near the center of the woods known as the "Old Cow Hole." Forrest believed that treasure was buried here. He once took a newsman to the area. The reporter described it as being a "small circular pool of gray water which seemed to swirl and yet was dead still." "This is where they buried the money," Forrest told him. "I think they must have killed a pirate and put him with it. There's everything in there. You hear chains rattle sometimes."

While Forrest claimed that he was not afraid of the dead, even though he believed that the dead come back, one experience he told of shook even him to the marrow:

> Once, I went out on a brilliant November night to shoot black ducks. I found a flock asleep on a little inlet where the pine trees came down to the edge of the water. As I raised my gun to fire, instead of them being ducks, I saw they were soldiers of the olden time. Headed by an officer, company after company of them formed and marched out of the water.
>
> Recovering from my astonishment, I ran to my skiff and tied up on the other side of the point. Arriving there, I found a man in uniform, his red coat showing brightly in the moonlight, sitting upright and very rigid in the stern. I was scared, but mad, too. So I yelled to him, "Get out of that skiff

or I'll shoot." "Shoot and the devil's curse to you and your traitor's breed," he answered, and made as if to strike me with the sword he carried. Then I drew my gun on him and pulled. It didn't go off. I pulled the trigger again. No better result. I dropped the gun and ran for home, and I'm not ashamed to say I swam the creek in doing it, too.

Forrest also used to tell of seeing a white ox lying in his cornfield one night:

I went out to drive him away. When I reached the spot where the animal was lying, I saw that it was a coffin covered with a sheet and borne along by invisible hands just at the height pallbearers would carry a corpse. I followed until it entered the woods. The sheet only partly covered the coffin. Well, sir, the following Wednesday they brought the body of Harry Daniels ashore from Wolf Trap lightship. Harry was killed when the boiler blew up. As the men carried him up the beach to the waiting hearse, I recognized instantly the coffin I had seen borne into Old House Woods!

Still another tale that has been printed in both newspapers and books involved a farmer's wife who lived adjacent to the woods. One evening, at dusk, she went into a pasture to bring home some workhorses. She drove them down a lane toward the barn. Arriving at the gate, she called to her husband to open it. He did not respond, and she opened it herself. As she did so, her husband came out of the barn and laughed at her, saying that he had put the team in the stable two hours before.

"Don't be foolish," she said. When she turned to let the team pass through the gate, instead of two horses standing there, she saw two headless black dogs scampering off toward Old House Woods. "That woman," says Olivia Davis, "was my great-grandmother." Over the years, there have also been numerous reported sightings of headless cattle wandering aimlessly in the woods.

Through the decades, there have been many mysterious disappearances in the region, involving both humans and animals. None has been satisfactorily explained. In 1950, Harry Forrest wrote of one:

It was near about 100 years ago that Lock Owens and Pidge Morgan came through these woods with their steer, on the way back from a cattle auction, and nothing's been seen of them since. Steer, carts and everything disappeared in there. Lock had a little black dog and the only thing that was ever found of it was a little bunch of hair off of that dog's tail.

There used to be a lot of cattle down on these points, but they got to wandering in here and never came out. Everything that comes in here heads for the Old Cow Hole and disappears. It's very strange. One night that old hole will be covered with water, the next evening it's dry. Some nights it'll be light enough to pick up a pin in the woods, and black and storming outside. And some, you'll come in here and it'll be pouring down. You get wringing wet, and then you come out and you'll be perfectly dry.

Finally, there is the tragic tale of Tom Pipkin, a local fisherman who lived in the vicinity about 1880. Fired up by the age-old stories of buried or sunken gold, he took his small boat into the woods, following an old channel—some say it was originally cut by pirates two centuries earlier—and headed for Old Cow Hole. Several days later, his boat was found in the bay. Inside the boat were two gold coins of unknown age and a battered silver cup covered with slime and mud. One coin bore a Roman head, and the letters "IVVS" were distinguishable. No one would take Pipkin's boat, and it rotted away on nearby Gwynn's Island. He was never heard from again.

"A thousand people have been in here after that money, but they'll never get it," Harry Forrest once said of Old House Woods. "The trees start bending double and howling. It storms, and they get scared and take off. The woods is haunted, that's what it is."

PART II
EASTERN SHORE AREA

THE GHOST SAMARITAN THAT SAVED A SHIP

The following is excerpted from Hereward Carrington's 1920 book, Phantasms of the Dead.

In 1664, Captain Thomas Rogers, commander of a ship called "The Society," was bound on a voyage from London to Tidewater Virginia. One day an observation was made. The mates and officers brought their books and cast up their reckonings with the captain, to see how near they were to the coast. They all agreed they were 100 leagues from the Capes of Virginia. Upon these customary reckonings, and heaving the lead, and finding no ground at 100 fathoms, they set the watch and the captain turned in. The weather was fine; a moderate gale of wind blew from the coast; so that the ship might have run about 12 or 13 leagues in the night after the captain was in his cabin.

He fell asleep, and slept very soundly for about three hours, when he woke, and lay still till he heard his second mate turn out and relieve the watch. He then called to his first mate, as he was going off watch, and asked him how all things fared. The mate answered that all was well, though the gale had freshened, and they were running at a great rate; but it was a fair wind, and a fair, clear night.

The captain then went to sleep again. About an hour after, he dreamed that someone was pulling him, and bade him turn out and look around. He, however, lay still and went to sleep once more; but was suddenly reawakened. This occurred several times; and, though he knew not what was the reason, yet he found it impossible to go to sleep anymore. Then he heard an unseen vision say, "Turn out and look around!"

The captain lay in this state of uneasiness nearly two hours, until, finally, he felt compelled to don his great coat and go on deck. All was well; it was a fine, clear night. The men saluted him; and he called out, "How's she heading?" "Southwest by south, sir," answered the mate; "fair for the coast, and the wind east by north."

"Very good," said the captain, and as he was about to return to his cabin, something he couldn't see stood by him and said, "Heave the lead!" Upon hearing this, the captain said to the second mate: "When did you heave the lead? What water have you?" "About an hour ago, sir," replied the mate; "60 fathoms."

"Heave again," the captain commanded. When the lead was cast they had ground at 11 fathoms! This surprised them all; but much more when, at the next cast, it came up seven fathoms. Upon this, the captain, in a fright, bid them to put the helm alee, and about ship, all hands ordered to back the sails, as is usual in such cases.

The proper orders being observed, the ship came about; but before the sails filled, she had but four fathoms and a half water under her stern. As soon as she filled and stood off, they had seven fathoms again, and at the next cast, 11 fathoms, and so on to 20 fathoms. They then stood off to seaward; all the rest of the watch, to get into deep water, till daybreak, when, being a clear morning, the Capes of Virginia were in fair view under their stern, and but a few leagues distant.

Had they stood on, but one cable length further, as they were going, they would have run aground and certainly lost their ship, if not their lives, all through the erroneous reckonings of the previous day. Who or what was it that waked the captain and bade him save the ship?

That, he has never been able to tell.

THE MYSTERY OF THE BLOODY MILLSTONE

"Oh, she's still around. We still hear from her every once in a while. We find things out of place, you know, where they shouldn't be. And the stain still appears on the stone every time it rains. She's still a part of the family."

Sam Nock is talking about the resident ghost at Warwick, the ancestral home of the Upshur family in the small town of Quinby in Accomack County on Virginia's Eastern Shore. Nock is a historian and a high school teacher here. The ghost is that of Rachel Upshur, who died a horribly tragic death on Christmas Day more than 250 years ago.

Nock says that Rachel married Abel Upshur in 1725, and they had five children. Abel was the grandson of Arthur Upshur, who had arrived on the Eastern Shore as a cabin boy sometime during the first half of the seventeenth century and rose to become one of the leading citizens of the area. Abel and Rachel moved to Warwick, one of the earliest brick houses still standing in the county, in 1738.

Eleven years later, on a bitter, blustery and rainy winter night, the couple was awakened by a loud commotion in their chicken house. Although he was ill at the time, Abel got up to check on the noise, even after Rachel begged him not to go. She told him that she had a terrifying nightmare in which a white-shrouded, grinning skeleton with upraised arms had solemnly warned her not to venture out of the house that evening. If she did, she would meet death in some horrible manner. Abel reassured her that everything would be all right and asked her to stay in bed.

But when he didn't return within a reasonable time, she became worried, hastily threw on a coat over her nightgown and went out to find out what had happened. She found Abel standing in the cold rain. The chickens were still making a racket, but he had not discovered why. She implored him to get back in the house.

As they walked to the door, Rachel stepped up on an old millstone that was embedded in the ground at the foot of the steps. As she did, a fox darted out from under the steps and sank its teeth into one of her heels. Blood spurted out on the millstone as she limped inside.

The fox was rabid, and a few days later Rachel contracted hydrophobia. There was no known cure at the time for this horrid ailment, which viciously attacks the nervous system causing a victim great pain, suffering and madness. Family members, with no choice but to put her out of her misery, smothered her to death between two feather mattresses. It was Christmas Day 1749. She was buried in the family plot at Warwick.

The old millstone is still there today. It is a solid gray, well-worn stone. Curiously, Nock declares, whenever it rains and the stone gets wet, a large, dark-red stain appears on the precise spot where Rachel bled when the fox bit her so long ago.

THE "ORDEAL OF TOUCH"

Superstition was rampant in Virginia, even before the famous witch trials occurred in Salem, Massachusetts. It was brought over to the New World with the settlers: ancient beliefs in the bizarre, handed down family to family for centuries in Europe.

One of the weirdest of these old rituals was known as the "Ordeal of Touch." For some unexplained reason, it was believed by some that if a murderer touched or came into the presence of the body of his or her victim, the wounds that had been inflicted on the victim would "bleed afresh." This archaic notion can be traced to seventeenth-century England and Scotland, where it was widely believed.

Even William Shakespeare was drawn into the tradition. He wrote the following in Act I, Scene II of *Richard III*, where Lady Anne, in the presence of the body of the dead king, is made to accuse Gloster in this passage:

> *O gentlemen, see, see, dead Henry's wounds*
> *Open their congeal'd mouths and bleed afresh!*
> *Blush, blush, thou lump of foul deformity,*
> *For't is thy presence that exhales this blood*
> *From cold and empty veins, where no blood dwells.*

There are at least two recorded instances of actual cases where the Ordeal of Touch occurred in the commonwealth. They have been documented in both history magazines and books. One such example is in the records of Northampton County: "On December 14, 1656, Captain William Whittington issued a warrant for a Jury of Inquest over the body of Paul Rynners," suspected to have been murdered by William Custis. The jury reported: "We have viewed the body of Paul Rynners, late of this county deceased & have caused Wm. Custis to touch the face and stroke the body of said Paul Rynners which he willingly did. But no sign did appear unto us of question in the law." Custis was freed.

The second incident involved the alleged murder of an infant, born of Mary Andrews of Accomack. Mary was the unmarried daughter of Sarah Carter and the stepdaughter of Paul Carter. Both Paul and Sarah were accused of the crime and brought to trial. The following is from Accomack court records:

Att a Court held and continued for Accomack County, March 18, 1679. The Confession of Paul Carter taken the First day of March 1679.

Question. What doe yu know concerning a child born of Mary the daughter of Sarah, the wife of the said Paul?

Answere. That he doth know that the said Mary had a man child born of her body and that the said Sarah assisted at the birth of the said child & that he certainly knoweth not whether it were born alive or not & that they did endeavor to preserve the life thereof and that it lay betwixt his wife and her daughter all night and that ye next morning he saw it dead & he and his wife carefully buried the said child but that his wife carefully washing and dressed it.

The body of the baby was exhumed so that it could be "stroaked" by the accused couple. A jury consisting of twelve women was seated. Paul Carter was found guilty of the crime, because while he was "stroaking" the child, "black and sotted places" on the body grew "fresh and red."

It was not specified what punishment Paul was given. This, however, is said to be the last instance of trial by Ordeal of Touch on record in Virginia.

PART III
WESTERN AREA

STRANGE LIGHTS IN THE NIGHT

Most forms of psychic phenomena are quite limited in scope. Generally, whatever the manifestation—be it the sighting of a milky apparition, the sound of muffled footsteps in the attic or a bloodstain that cannot be scrubbed clean—the particular characteristic is experienced only by a relatively few people. In most cases only one person, usually psychically sensitive, is involved. Often in old ancestral homes just the immediate family members encounter the extraordinary. Only in rare instances are the occurrences seen, heard, smelled, felt or tasted by appreciable numbers of people.

That is why the mysterious light at West Point, Virginia, west of Williamsburg, is such an unusual example of unexplained phenomena. Over the past one hundred years or so, literally thousands of Tidewater residents swear that they have witnessed the light that appears and disappears before their eyes. In fact, this sensation is so well known and so reliable in its recurrences that for decades area teenagers considered it a cool thing to drive to the site late at night and wait for it to show up. As often as not, they were not disappointed. It is a legend that has been retold from generation to generation, with many common threads but with conflicting accounts as to the actual source.

Skeptics scoff that what is seen is marsh gas, which is common in the area near West Point at a crossroads called Cohoke. Others say that many of those who come looking for the light are well fortified with "liquid courage" and are likely to see anything. But the majority of those who have been there don't buy these explanations.

"There definitely is a light there," says Mac Germain, a local mechanic. "I've seen it and I wasn't drunk and it wasn't marsh gas. If it was swamp gas then why would people have seen the light at all times of the year?"

"I've seen it and it's real," claims Mrs. Thomas Whitmore of West Point. "It was so bright. When it got close to us we got off the railroad tracks real fast, but nothing came by." Ed Jenkins of Gloucester says, "We used to go up there when we were teenagers. It was the thing to do. I saw it. It would come closer and closer and would almost get to you, then it would vanish. Was I scared? Absolutely! One time I shot at it with a shotgun and it disappeared. But it always came back."

"I've seen it a hundred times," says John Waggoner of Newport News. "It was just a big old light, and it came straight down the tracks, but when it got to you there was nothing there. It used to scare the hell out of the girls I took there. That's what I liked about it."

One person who firmly ruled out any spectral source was the late Lon Dill, a local historian who wrote extensively of the area. "Oh, there is something there," he said. "There is a light, but it is some form of luminescence which can be caused in several ways. Your eyes can fool you at times, especially at night." Another person who has tried to downplay the supernatural aspects of the light is former King William County sheriff W.W. Healy. He recalls that in the 1960s and 1970s "[i]t was almost like a state fair down there. People would come by the carload to see it. It got to the point where the road was blocked." Healy did his best to discourage curiosity seekers.

Maggie Wolfe, a former reporter for the *Virginia Gazette* in Williamsburg, tells of the time when she and her husband were driving by the area late at night: "We were taking some back roads, and when we got near West Point I got the strangest feeling that is hard to describe. It was overpowering, as if we were in the midst of a superstrong presence. We were paralleling the railroad tracks, and when we looked over, there was this light. It seemed to be following us. And then it was gone. There was no train, no noise or anything."

Bruce Johnson is a local farmer who grew up in the Cohoke vicinity and still lives there. His father's farm is within a stone's throw of where the light is most often seen. "A lot of people have gone to see it," he says. "I've seen license plates from all over the country. It seems like it is most frequently seen on cloudy or rainy, dismal nights. I only saw it once. I was driving home alone. I stopped at the tracks, and I definitely saw some type of light. It had a gaseous-type glow. Actually, it was kind of scary. I didn't stay long."

Most everyone who has seen the light is pretty much in agreement as to its method of appearance. It first shows up far off, maybe several hundred yards down the tracks. Then, noiselessly, it approaches, glaring ever brighter as it nears, until its frightening closeness scares off viewers. Its relentless journey can only be impeded by the foolhardy actions of those who either try to run it down or shoot at it. Also, although many have tried, including a national magazine film crew, no one has successfully photographed the light.

The source of the light, however, remains a mystery and stirs heated arguments. Many believe in the "lost train" theory. They have heard that after an 1864 battle near Richmond during the Civil War, a train was loaded with wounded Confederate soldiers and dispatched to West Point, where they could recuperate. The train left Richmond amid a soft chorus of moans but never reached its destination.

The train theory was given some support by the experience of the late Tom Gulbranson and members of his family in 1967. Tom was an amateur psychic sleuth who investigated scores of alleged haunted houses and sites. He had visited the Cohoke location several times and had seen the light during a few of them. This time he was with his mother, father, brother and a friend.

As they drove up and parked at a strategic point, they noticed another car that had parked on the tracks opposite of them. Tom got out his camera and tape recorder equipment, set them up and waited. It was a bitterly cold night, and after four hours of nothing but silence and darkness, they decided to leave. Just as they were packing up, the light appeared.

"This time it was brighter than I had ever seen it," Tom recalled. "It was an intense light, and it came closer and closer. As it neared, the other parked car's occupants flicked on their headlights, and when that happened, we all clearly saw the outline of a locomotive engine pass by!"

Apparently, whatever mission the ghost train is on, it hasn't yet been fulfilled because stories of the eerie light persist to this day.

The Brakeman's Lantern

Not to be outdone, residents of Suffolk, near Norfolk and Virginia Beach, say that they have their own spectral light and their own railroad tradition behind it. This, too, is a story that has been around a long time. Its setting is a bleak stretch of railroad tracks on the outskirts of the Great Dismal Swamp near Jackson Road, a gloomy and deserted lane close to the North Carolina border.

Larry Parker, an insurance agent who grew up in Suffolk, remembers seeing the light one night. "It lasted only a few seconds," he says, "but it felt like days. It was right on top of us. It lit up the front of the car and then was gone. It could be a will-o'-the-wisp, which is a cloud of swamp gas that can become fluorescent under certain atmospheric conditions. All I know is that for sure there is something out there. I've seen it a dozen times." Others have said that the light sort of "danced" down the tracks and that from a distance it looked like an old-fashioned lantern.

"It just appeared all of a sudden out of the trees," says Raleigh Isaacs Jr., who lives about two miles from the site. "It was big and bright and moved up and down beside the rails, as if someone was waving it. We watched it once for about an hour before it blinked out." The light is most often sighted in late summer or early fall.

The prevalent rumors pertaining to the origin of the light swirl around an unidentified railroad brakeman who, long ago, during a heavy storm, tried to signal the engineer that a tree had fallen across the tracks. Unseen in the rain and fog, the man was struck and his head was decapitated.

According to Brad Rock, a Suffolk native and a member of the Tidewater Chapter of the National Railway Historical Society, "That brakeman has been doomed to wander the tracks forever searching for his head."

THE HAUNTED PORTRAIT

It is unquestionably one of the most magnificent original colonial mansions in the United States. Architectural historians believe that parts of its impressive design were inspired by the governor's palace in Williamsburg. The site on which the great house sits is steeped in early Virginia history and tradition. It was, in fact, built in 1613, just six years after the first settlers landed at nearby Jamestown and a full seven years before the pilgrims arrived at Plymouth Rock.

This is Shirley Plantation, located at a point overlooking a scenic bend in the James River about halfway between Williamsburg and Richmond. It

Historic Shirley Plantation in Charles City County, west of Williamsburg, is the house in which the haunted portrait of "Aunt Pratt" hangs.

was originally owned by Sir Thomas West, the first royal governor of the Colony of Virginia. He named it in honor of his wife's father, Sir Thomas Sherley of Whitson, England. The estate later gained eminence as the home of Colonel Edward Hill, who held many high offices in the colony through the mid-seventeenth century. The property has been in the Hill and Carter families for more than three hundred years.

The present house was begun in 1723 by the third Edward Hill. It took nearly fifty years to complete the construction and was done, as one author described it, "with a lavish disregard for cost seldom displayed in the building of great mansions." This handsome brick house stands three stories, with rows of dormer windows projecting from the roof on all sides. It has huge twin chimneys, which flank a large carved pineapple, the symbol of colonial hospitality. Two splendid two-story porticos, each with four white pillars, set off the front of the building with stylish grace.

Inside, eighteenth-century artisans fashioned superb paneling and delicate carvings. A major design feature is an elegant carved walnut staircase that rises for three stories without visible support, the only one of its kind in America. The entire house is filled with exquisite furnishings, crested silver and interesting memorabilia assembled from the many generations of the families who have lived here.

Shirley was a well-known center of hospitality a century before and during the Revolutionary War. George Washington and Thomas Jefferson were guests, as were numerous other prominent Virginians. One of the most charming anecdotes that took place in the house occurred late in the eighteenth century when a young and beautiful Anne Hill Carter was carrying a punchbowl across the dining room, and it began to slip from her fingers. She was rescued by a dashing young military officer, "Light Horse" Harry Lee. Not long afterward they were married at Shirley. Their son became one of the most famous of all Virginians: Robert E. Lee.

Perhaps the most intriguing legend at the plantation revolves around the ghost of a former resident and family member, a woman known as "Aunt Pratt." She reportedly was a sister of Edward Hill and was born late in the seventeenth century. Little is known of her, but it is said that there always was a certain air of mystery about the woman. One of the things Shirley is noted for is its fine collection of family portraits. Aunt Pratt's picture occupied a prominent place in a downstairs bedroom for a number of years after her death. Then, in the 1960s, as a new generation of the family took over occupancy and decided to redecorate, her portrait was taken down and banished to the obscurity of the attic.

Aunt Pratt, or rather her spirit, did not take kindly to this. In fact, she made what household members described as a "mighty disturbance." This usually took the form of the sound of a woman crying and rocking in the attic late at night. A number of guests, as well as the Hills and Carters, told of hearing the incessant rocking on certain nights. Yet when they summoned courage to check the attic, all was still and quiet. Nothing was amiss. Eventually, the restlessness of her spirit proved too much for the residents, and they prudently brought the portrait back down and hung it in its rightful place. Once this was done, the strange sounds were never heard again.

This, however, did not end Aunt Pratt's troubles. In 1971, and this is documented, the Virginia State Travel Council scoured the commonwealth in search of relics, antiques and other items associated with psychic phenomena for a tourist promotion it was assembling in New York City. Council officials, having heard the story of Aunt Pratt's ghostly rocking, asked if they might borrow the portrait for the exhibit. And so "she" was crated and shipped north. But no sooner had she been hung on a wall when she once again "came to life," openly venting her displeasures at being so far away from home.

According to credible witness accounts, the portrait was once observed "swinging" in its display case. Then, one morning, workmen found the portrait lying on the floor, several feet away from the case and, in their words, "heading toward the exit." As a security measure, officials had Aunt Pratt locked up in a closet when not on exhibit. One night, a maintenance crew became unnerved when they heard "knocking and crying" coming from the locked closet. No one was inside. The next morning, the portrait mysteriously had escaped from the closet and was lying on the floor outside.

Psychic experts are in general agreement that spirits that manifest themselves in the manner Aunt Pratt did are actually ghosts of residents who believe, even though they are long dead and gone, that the house they lived in still belongs to them. This seems to be the most plausible explanation in Aunt Pratt's case. Subsequent events added credence to this theory. On its way back south from the New York showing, the portrait was taken to a shop in Richmond, Virginia, so that repairs could be made on the now battered frame. When it was picked up later, the shop owner said that ever since Aunt Pratt had been in his care he heard bells ringing. This he deemed at best odd and at worst eerily haunting because, he added, there were no bells of any kind in his shop.

The portrait was then restored once more to its proper place on a wall in the downstairs bedroom, and Aunt Pratt has not been heard from again— with one startling exception.

The portrait of "Aunt Pratt" at Shirley Plantation is said to be haunted whenever it is removed from its preferred place on the wall of a bedroom.

A few years ago, the author was called by one of Shirley's historical interpreters. She said that she had been telling the story of Aunt Pratt to a group of tourists. One man who was standing in front of a large chest right beneath the portrait said, "That the biggest bunch of baloney I ever heard." At that precise instant, the doors of the chest suddenly sprang open and banged him sharply on his backside! The interpreter said that the room emptied in ten seconds.

THE SAD SPIRIT OF WESTOVER

Two large metallic eagles adorn the gateposts leading into Westover Plantation, in Charles City County, set majestically along a beautiful stretch of the James River about halfway between Williamsburg and Richmond. Westover is considered an outstanding example of Georgian architecture in America. Built early in the eighteenth century, it was, for generations, the ancestral home of the William Byrd family, one of the most powerful and influential clans in the colonies.

Westover Plantation in Charles City County was the home of Evelyn Byrd more than two centuries ago. Her ghost, roaming the grounds, has been seen over the years by multiple witnesses.

Westover was the scene of lavish social entertainment among the more affluent colonists during the 1700s. Great parties were held here, with the rich and famous as frequent guests. But the house is also associated with a history of loneliness, sadness and tragedy and for centuries has earned a reputation for being haunted.

If there is such a thing as a benevolent ghost, or at least one that is dedicated not to frighten those who encounter it, then there is perhaps no better example than the gentle, fragile spirit of Evelyn Byrd of Westover. Though she has been dead for more than 250 years, her apparition continues to occasionally reappear in the house and on the grounds: a wraithlike figure most often dressed in white, sad and haunting, as if still seeking the happiness that eluded her in life.

Born in 1707, she was a bright child, a bit spoiled, precocious and high spirited. She was the daughter of William Byrd II—master of Westover, one of the most prominent statesmen of his time, secretary of the Virginia colony, founder of the city of Richmond, wealthy landowner and country squire.

When Evelyn was just ten, her father took her to England so she could be properly schooled. There, she flowered into a beautiful young woman with porcelain-white skin; shining chestnut hair; slanting, almost Oriental blue-green eyes; and an enigmatic, Mona Lisa–like smile. It is told that when she was presented at court at age sixteen, the king of England remarked: "I am not surprised why our young men are going to Virginia if there are so many pretty Byrds there."

It was in London where Evelyn fell deeply in love with a handsome Englishman. Most historians believe that he was Charles Morduant, the grandson of Lord Peterborough. Her father violently objected to the romance, telling her that if she proceeded with it, "[a]s to any expectation you may fondly entertain of a fortune from me, you are not to look for one brass farthing. Nay, beside all that, I will avoid the sight of you as a creature detested."

And so, against the desires of her heart, Evelyn Byrd returned to Westover in 1726 a changed young woman. The spark of her personality was diminished, and she spent long hours by herself, withdrawn and reclusive. A number of potential suitors from nearby plantations paid her visits over the next few years, but she spurned them all, much to the chagrin of her father. He referred to her as the "antique virgin."

She confided only in her close friend, Anne Carter Harrison, of neighboring Berkeley Plantation. They would walk in the formal gardens and talk among the giant boxwoods, passing the afternoons away. It was amid a poplar grove one day that the two young ladies made a secret pact: whoever died first would try to return to visit "in such a fashion not to frighten anyone." Did Evelyn have a premonition? Soon after, she passed away, some say of a broken heart.

On her tombstone was inscribed the following:

Here in the sleep of peace reposes the body of Evelyn Byrd, daughter of the Honorable William Byrd. The various and excellent endowments of nature: improved and perfected by an accomplished education formed her, for the happiness of her friends; for the ornament of her country. Alas Reader! We can detain nothing, however valued, from unrelenting death. Beauty, fortune, or valued honour! So here a proof! And be reminded by this awful tomb that every worldly comfort fleets away. Excepting only, what arises from imitating the virtues of our friends and the contemplation of their happiness. To which, God was pleased to call this Lady on the 13th day of November, 1737, in the 29th year of her age.

For months, the saddened Anne Harrison did not venture among the trails and trees that she and Evelyn had so often walked together. But one day, she

A portrait of Miss Evelyn Byrd of Westover Plantation in Charles City County. Though she died nearly three centuries ago, her spirit is still occasionally sighted roaming the estate grounds.

finally did go to the poplar grove and felt "a presence." She turned and saw a figure approaching. It was Evelyn. It is said that she was "dressed in white, dazzling in ethereal loveliness. She drifted a few steps, kissed her hand to the beholder, smiled happily, and vanished."

Over the intervening generations, others have caught fleeting glimpses of Evelyn, among them former Westover owners and guests. In 1856, for example, one woman told the family of John Selden, who then lived at the mansion, that she had awakened in the night and found a young lady standing in the room who quickly went out the door. She described the lady and her dress. "Oh, yes," Mr. Selden remarked, "that was Evelyn Byrd." In the early 1900s, a craftsman was dispatched to do some repair work in the same bedroom. Minutes later, he came running down the stairs, saying to the owner, "You didn't tell me there was a young lady up there." He had seen her combing her hair before a mirror. When they went back upstairs, there was no one there.

In December 1929, a guest of the family of Richard Crane, who then owned the plantation, reported seeing the "filmy, nebulous and cloudy figure of a woman, so transparent no features could be distinguished, only the gauzy texture of a woman's form." It seemed, the guest said, "to be floating a little above the lawn." When the Cranes bought Westover in about 1920, Mrs. Crane said, "Oh dear, we'll never get any help because of the ghost." But they had no trouble, because even though the legend of Evelyn's reappearances was well known throughout the county, servants believed her to be a friendly spirit.

More recently, Mr. Bagby, who lived in a small house between the mansion and the cemetery where Evelyn is buried, was in his kitchen one evening when he saw a woman at eye level outside on the lawn. Thinking that it was Mrs. Bruce Crane Fisher, then mistress of Westover, he went outside to say hello. There was no one there. Then, remembering that his kitchen is raised, he realized that if he had seen the woman at eye level, she would have had to be at least ten feet tall!

Of all who have claimed sightings of Evelyn, though, no one yet has offered a reasonable explanation as to why her restless spirit would want to periodically return to a place that apparently had caused her so much unhappiness in life. Could it possibly be that Evelyn comes back to let it be known that she has been reunited with her English lover—that she has found in death the bliss she had been denied in life?

A TRAGIC TOAST AT BRANDON

It has been written about Brandon Plantation that "[i]t does not seem possible that so much loveliness can belong to one old house." Boxwood hedges, more than two centuries old, flank this superb manor home on a 4,500-acre

Brandon Plantation, on the south side of the James River, southwest of Surry, was the site of the tragic death of a young bride long ago, whose spirit still haunts the grounds.

farm located in Prince George County on the south side of the James River between Surry and Hopewell. The estate actually dates to 1616, when a vast grant of land was made to Captain William Martin, who accompanied John Smith on the first voyage to Virginia in 1607. The main part of the house was built about 1765 by Nathaniel Harrison II as a wedding present for his son, Benjamin, who was a friend of Thomas Jefferson. It is believed that Jefferson designed the center structure.

During the latter part of the eighteenth century, and for most of the nineteenth, Brandon was a prime site for the gala social life enjoyed by wealthy plantation owners of the times. Lavish parties, dances and weddings were held here, and the well-known gentlemen and ladies arrived in ornate coaches and by boat from the north side of the river from such great mansions as Shirley, Berkeley and Westover. It was from such an aura of refined gaiety that the main character in what evolved into a haunting tragedy emerged.

Her name was Jane Evelyn Harrison, the eighteen-year-old daughter of William Byrd Harrison of Williamsburg. She has been described as a charming heiress endowed with position and beauty. According to Hubert Davis, who documented the era, she "used her capricious blue eyes, winning smile, and every feminine wile she could summon to entrap and smash the hearts of young men." She was, in a sense, a real-life Scarlett O'Hara.

It was at a typically jubilant spring dance at Brandon that Jane met and immediately entranced a young Frenchman named Pierre Bondurant. He instantly fell hopelessly in love with the fickle belle and repeatedly proposed marriage to her. By applying an intriguing feminine mystique beyond her years, she left Pierre more or less dangling. She told him, as he was leaving for a lengthy trip to Paris, that such a union would only be possible with the expressed approval of her father, knowing full well that this would be all but impossible. Pierre was persistent, suggesting that they elope to France, but Jane demurred, saying that she planned to spend the summer at Brandon, partying with friends.

Saddened but ever hopeful, Pierre departed for Paris. He had hardly been there a month when he received a letter from a friend, the news of which devastatingly tore at his very fiber. William Byrd Harrison had announced the engagement of Jane. She was to wed Ralph Fitzhugh Cocke of Bacon's Castle in late November. The wedding was to be held at Brandon so as to accommodate more than one hundred guests, ironically including Pierre Bondurant. And so, on the last day of November, a sumptuous feast was held, featuring the finest foods and the best wines and liquors in the commonwealth.

The wedding took place at 4:00 p.m. and was followed by an extravagant reception. At some point during the festivities, Pierre, curiously, pulled Jane aside, handed her a glass of champagne and asked her to exchange toasts with him. Delighted that he seemed to show no lingering bitterness from their past fling, she agreed, and they each drank to the other's happiness. Just then, the groom walked up, unnoticed by the couple, and overheard Pierre offer a strange poem to Jane. "Twas you I loved when we first met, I loved you then and I love you yet; 'Tis vain for me to try to forget, Lo! Both of us could die before sunset!"

Obviously embarrassed when he realized that Ralph had heard him, Pierre gulped down his champagne, made excuses and nervously left the house. By the time all but the house guests had gone, Jane had become deathly ill and had collapsed on the drawing room floor, gasping for breath. She was whisked to an upstairs bedroom and died that evening. Although it wasn't known then, she had been poisoned. A veil of silence and sadness descended on everyone.

Oddly, as Jane's body was being prepared for burial, it was noticed that her wedding ring was missing. No one could shed any light on this mystery, and she was laid to rest. A few days later, a messenger arrived from Williamsburg with the shocking news that Pierre Bondurant had been found dead in his carriage when it arrived in Williamsburg on the night of the wedding. Even more discomforting was the fact that Jane's wedding ring had been found—in Pierre's pocket!

The mistress of Brandon—Elizabeth Richardson Harrison, Jane's aunt—in an extraordinarily peculiar gesture, declared that the ring now bore a curse, and she had it embedded into the plaster on the ceiling above the spot where Jane had fallen.

Over the years following, there were periodic reports from residents, guests and servants of seeing the wispy apparition of a young woman, in a flowing white wedding gown, who seemed to appear only in late November, and Brandon slowly began gaining a reputation as being haunted. In fact, when Helen Lynne Thomas became mistress of the plantation, fully two generations after the tragedy, the real estate agent had casually referred to a "resident ghost."

That fall, Helen met the spectral being firsthand. It was on a stormy dark night as she was walking past the family cemetery. Amid the weathered old tombstones, she got a glimpse of a wraithlike figure drifting toward the main house. She trembled with fear, nearly fainted and then regained her composure and hurried into the great hall. There she heard a thud that sounded like something heavy had fallen in the adjacent drawing room. She walked across the hall, opened the door and saw that some plaster had fallen from the ceiling.

Then, as her eyes adjusted to the darkness, she saw something else—the same ethereal, white-clad phantom she had imagined she had seen outside. It appeared to hover about the room for a few seconds and then settled over the pile of plaster, as if it were searching for something. Helen could hardly breathe. Then, either the door or a loose floorboard creaked, and the figure straightened up, slid toward the door and disappeared.

As it did, Helen screamed and fainted dead away. When she was aroused, more than an hour later, she told members of her family and the servants who had rushed to her what had happened. It was then that one of the servants, Hattie McCoy, told her about Jane Harrison and Pierre Bondurant. Hattie's grandmother had been at Brandon on the fateful wedding day.

After she recovered, Helen sorted through the fallen plaster and found a "blackened, tarnished wedding ring!" She had it suspended from the ceiling from a small wire several inches long. It can still be seen there today.

BIZARRE TWISTS AT BACON'S CASTLE

It was, to the Virginia colonists, an ominous sign of impending disaster. It occurred sometime during the latter months of 1675. A great comet appeared in the sky, sweeping across the heavens and trailing a bright orange tail of fire. Soon after this eerie phenomenon came the flight of tens of thousands of passenger pigeons. For days they blanketed the horizon, blotting out the sun. Then, in the spring of 1676, a plague of locusts ravaged the colony, devouring every plant in sight and stripping trees of their leaves.

To the colonists, the comet was the worst sign. Many remembered that another comet had streaked across the Virginia skies just before the terrible Indian massacre of 1644. Believing in spectral omens, it was thus no surprise to them when, the following year, one of the bloodiest and most notorious chapters of the commonwealth's history was written.

It began on a quiet summer Sunday: some colonists passing by the Stafford County plantation of Thomas Mathew on their way to church discovered the overseer, Robert Hen, lying in a pool of blood. Nearby lay an Indian servant, dead. Hen also was mortally wounded, but before he expired, he managed to gasp, "Doegs! Doegs!" The words struck fear into the hearts of the passersby, for Hen had mentioned the name of a tribe of Indians known for their fierce attacks on white men and women.

The Doeg raid was executed in retaliation for the killing of several Indians by planters who had caught them stealing pigs and other livestock. Such raids were not new to the settlers. They had been periodically besieged ever since they first landed in Jamestown in 1607. This latest episode proved to be the last straw for many. For years they had sought action by the aristocratic governor of the colony at the time, Sir William Berkeley, but he was reluctant to move. And so the seeds were sown for what was to lead to the largest and most violent insurrection of the colonial era up to that time: Bacon's Rebellion.

Dashing Nathaniel Bacon, twenty-eight years old, had arrived in Virginia only three years earlier. Well educated and well endowed, he has been described by biographers as a slender, attractive, dark-haired man with an impetuous, sometimes fiery, temperament and a persuasive tongue. Above all else, Bacon was a natural leader of men. While Governor Berkeley remained inactive and inattentive in Jamestown, planters sought out Bacon to lead retaliatory strikes against the marauding Indians. When his own plantation was attacked and his overseer killed, Bacon agreed. He proved to be a skilled and capable military commander. On one march, his forces drove the Pamunkey tribe deep into Dragon's Swamp. Later, Bacon and his forces overpowered the Susquehannocks, killing at least one hundred Indians and capturing others.

Berkeley, furious at the unauthorized attacks launched by the rebellious group, dispatched his own troops to capture Bacon and his men. For the next several weeks, the two men waged a cat-and-mouse game that involved daring, intrigue and bloodshed. At one point, Bacon surrendered, was brought before Berkeley and was forgiven when he repented. But then he escaped, returned with a force of six hundred men and captured Jamestown, demanding a commission to fight the Indians, as well as the repeal of some harsh colonial laws. With no other choice under the show of arms, Berkeley granted the wishes, but when Bacon set out again chasing Indians, the governor repudiated all agreements and sent his troops after the rebels.

After several skirmishes, Bacon recaptured Jamestown and had it sacked and burned to the ground. Berkeley, who had retreated to the Eastern Shore of Virginia, meanwhile, was regrouping his forces for a final and decisive confrontation. It never came to pass. Bacon, who had suffered an attack of malaria at Jamestown, fell critically ill in Gloucester and died of dysentery there on October 26, 1676, at the age of twenty-nine. With the leader lost,

Historic Bacon's Castle, near Surry, has been the site of multiple psychic manifestations over the years, including a haunting fireball that travels between the building and a nearby cemetery.

the rebellion fell apart, and Berkeley's forces captured many of Bacon's men. A large number of them were hanged, continuing for several more months, the tragedy being forewarned by the appearance of the comet.

For three months in 1676, about seventy of Bacon's followers occupied a large brick mansion in Surry County, just across the James River from Jamestown. Then called "Allen's Brick House," it has been known, ever since this occupancy, as "Bacon's Castle." Now operated by the Association for the Preservation of Virginia Antiquities, this imposing brick structure was built sometime after 1655. It stands amid a large grove of oak trees. There are two expansive, paneled first-floor rooms, two more rooms on the second floor and what has been described as a dungeonlike attic on the third.

Accounts of ghostly hauntings at the castle have been passed along, generation to generation, for more than three hundred years. Some of those who have experienced strange sightings, noises and "presences" believe that they are manifestations of the devil. Others feel they may be the spectral return of Bacon's supporters, still seeking redress of the grievances they held against Governor Berkeley and the colony so many years ago. Whatever the case, it is an undisputed fact that the happenings that have occurred at the castle through the centuries have taken many forms.

Consider the revelations of Mrs. Charles Walker Warren, whose family once owned the mansion. When she was a young woman, early in the twentieth century, a visiting Baptist preacher who was spending the night stayed up late reading his Bible. Sometime in the wee hours of the morning, he heard footsteps descending the stairs from the second floor. He later said that someone or something had opened the parlor door and walked past him. He saw no one but felt the strong sensation that he was not alone. Then, mysteriously, a red velvet–covered rocking chair began moving back and forth as if someone were sitting in it, though the preacher could see no one. He put down his Bible and shouted, "Get thee behind me, Satan!" and the rocking abruptly stopped.

Mrs. Warren and a number of guests reported hearing footsteps on the stairs late at night many times. One visitor distinctly heard "horrible moaning" in the attic directly above her bedroom, though she was assured the next morning that no mortal could have been in the attic. On another occasion, Mrs. Warren came into the downstairs parlor one morning and found that the glass globe from a favorite nickel-plated reading lamp had shattered into tiny fragments yet, strangely, not a drop of kerosene from it had spilled onto the carpet. Also, a leather-bound dictionary had been flung across the room onto a sofa, and the iron stand on which it normally rested had been hurled to a distant corner. No rational explanation could be offered to clear this up.

Richard Reynolds, curator of the castle from 1973 to 1981, used to tell of the time one morning at 3:30 a.m. when he was awakened by the sound of his two-year-old son laughing in his crib in an upstairs bedroom. "Daddy, where's the lady?" the child asked Reynolds when he reached him. "What lady?" Reynolds said. "The lady with the white hands. She was tickling me." On another occasion a few years later, a tour guide was standing in the great hall one morning, before the castle was opened to the public for the day, when "something" ran by her from the outside passageway and went through the hall into another chamber on the other side. She heard feet running on the hardwood floor but did not see anyone. As the sound of the steps was passing by, something brushed her arm and gave her a chill. The same hostess also said that there had been strange noises a number of times, most commonly loud popping and crackling sounds, which sometimes were heard by people in the reception room. They were too much for one young couple, who became so frightened that they left the castle even before the tour had started.

These and several other incidents, however, serve merely as preambles to the most shocking supernatural appearance at Bacon's Castle, one that has reappeared regularly at varying intervals over the years and has been seen and documented by a number of credible witnesses from several different generations. It takes the form, say those who have seen and been terrified by it, of a "pulsating red ball of fire." It apparently rises near or from the graveyard of Old Lawne's Creek Church, a few hundred yards south of the castle, soars about thirty to forty feet in the air, always on dark nights, and then moves slowly northward. It seems to float or hover above the castle grounds and sometimes enters an upstairs window before moving back toward the ivy-covered walls of the ruins of the church, where it disappears.

One eyewitness, G.I. Price, a former caretaker at the castle, described the phenomenon to a local newspaper reporter this way: "I was standing, waiting in the evening for my wife to shut up the chickens, when a light about the size of a jack-me-lantern came out of the old loft door and went up a little, traveling by floating along about 40 feet in the air toward the direction of the old graveyard."

Skeptics, of course, contend that the fireball is merely some form of physical manifestation that can be explained scientifically. But those who have seen it, including members of the Warren family and others, could never be convinced that it was not of a mystical, spiritual nature. Some even called it an appearance of the "Prince of Darkness." One guest reportedly had the wits frightened out of him one night when the fiery red ball sailed into his bedroom at the castle, circled over his bed several times and then disappeared out an open window.

A former owner of the mansion told of seeing the fireball blaze overhead and enter his barn. Fearful of it igniting his stored hay, he ran toward the barn. Then the bright, glowing light turned and headed back to the graveyard. In the 1930s, members of a local Baptist church, meeting at an evening revival session, collectively saw the paranormal sphere. It is said that the praying that night was more intense than ever before in the congregation's memory.

What is the origin of this eerie fireball, and why does it reappear every so often? One legend offered is that a servant a century or so ago was late with his chores, and as he was walking home in the darkness, the red object overcame him, burst and covered him with a hellish mass of flames, burning him to death. Another theory is that the light is somehow tied to hidden treasure in the castle. Some money was found there years ago when two men were removing some bricks from the fireplace hearth on the second floor.

Many old-timers, however, prefer to believe that the fireball is a periodic reminder of the brilliant comet that flashed across the same skies more than three hundred years ago, forewarning that tragedy and bloodshed would soon follow. There are, in fact, those who are convinced that spirits frequent Bacon's Castle to this day—sad spirits from long ago, still seeking relief from their troubled and grief-stricken past.

THE "CURSE TREE" OF JAMESTOWN ISLAND

Just beyond Jamestown Memorial Church, which was built in 1907 upon the foundation of an original church erected in 1617, is a small, quiet, tree-shaded cemetery containing only a handful of graves. It is here where James and Sarah Harrison Blair are buried. Dr. Blair was, in the late seventeenth century, one of the leading citizens of the Virginia colony and was the chief force behind the founding of the College of William and Mary, the second-oldest institution of higher learning in the country.

In 1687, Sarah Harrison, by popular accounts, was a strikingly beautiful young lady of seventeen who was an active participant in the social circle of plantation life along the lower James River. She has been described as

Above: The "Curse Tree" of Jamestown Island. Here, a large sycamore tree grew between the grave sites of James Blair and his young wife, Sarah, separating the couple after death. *Courtesy of the Association for the Preservation of Virginia Antiquities.*

Below: After the original "Curse Tree" of Jamestown Island was cut down, a second tree sprang up, continuing to push the grave sites of James Blair and his wife, Sarah, farther apart.

vivacious, full of life and headstrong. She was actively wooed by a number of young suitors but spurned them all when she met Blair, who was said to have swept her off her feet.

Her parents, however, were not so enchanted. There was a problem. Blair was thirty-one, nearly double Sarah's age, and her mother and father were dead set against such a union and tried everything to break up the couple. But Sarah persisted and the marriage took place. Shortly after that, her parents, tragically, were killed in a lightning storm.

Sarah and James Blair lived a happy life together, although it was cut short when she died in 1713 at the age of forty-two, and because of her feud with the family, she was buried behind the Jamestown Church instead of at the Harrison family cemetery. Dr. Blair lived on for thirty more years, and when he passed, in 1743, he was laid to rest at a site six inches to the left of his wife's grave.

Seven years later, fate intervened when a sycamore tree sapling sprang up between the couple's tombstones. As it grew, it began to push the two stones apart from each other, crumbling them as it did. And so, a legend was born. It was believed by many that Sarah's parents, who were unsuccessful in separating the two lovers in life, were doing so after death!

Robert L. Ripley wrote about the bizarre incident in his "Believe It or Not!" column, calling the sycamore the "mother-in-law tree." Others refer to it as the "curse tree." In the early 1900s, the old tree, which had grown to enormous size, was cut down and removed from the site, although the broken bricks and cracked tombs were left as they were, separated.

Within a few years, a second sycamore sapling sprang up in the exact same spot where the original tree had stood, and it flourishes today, continuing to push the Blair tombstones farther and farther apart.

A COLONIAL TIME WARP

The following extraordinary psychic encounter was experienced by Gerry McDowell and her late husband, Gus, in 1971. They both liked to travel and often visited interesting sites in the off-season. It was on such an excursion to Jamestown Island when it happened. They were there very early on a chilly autumn morning because, as Gerry says, "We liked to be out when no one was around so we could enjoy the solitude, and Gus liked to feed the animals." The story is best told in Gerry's own words.

I can remember it as clearly as if it happened yesterday. It was real early on a Sunday morning, about 6:00 a.m. It was damp and misty. You could see the fog rolling in off the James River. I was listening to one of those audio recordings which told all about the early settlement, when I had the strangest sensation. There was a deathly stillness in the air.

I turned around and there, coming down a path toward us was a group of about twenty people—men, women and children. They were all dressed in colonial costumes. The men wore knickers with either black or white stockings and shoes with buckles. They had on jacket blouses with white collars and very broad-brimmed hats. The ladies were wearing long gray or black dresses with shawls over their shoulders and bonnets.

They were very animated. The men and women were talking and laughing and waving their arms as they walked. The children were running in and out of the group. I thought at first that it might be a troupe of actors who were coming to participate in a play or something. I looked at Gus, and he saw them, too. We stood together and watched as they approached us.

It was then that we realized there was something different. While they seemed to be talking, there was no sound whatsoever. Instead, there was only an icy silence. They didn't appear to be ghosts, because I think most ghosts are wispy or transparent, and they weren't. You couldn't see through them. And then we noticed. They were ghosts because they were not walking on the ground! They were elevated above it by a few inches.

Gus and I froze. We stood still and didn't say a thing. We felt together that any movement or sound on our part would dissolve them. On they came. They marched right by us without noticing us. It was as if we weren't there. We could have reached out and touched them, but we didn't. They moved past us and walked straight up to the path to the old church. When we turned to follow them, we could barely believe our eyes. The church had transformed from its present state to how it must have looked in the early 1600s, complete with steeple and all! Gus and I both gasped.

They opened the door and, one by one, went inside. When the last gentleman entered, he turned and appeared to stare at us. Gus said he had a smile on his face. He slammed the door forcefully. Again, there was no sound. We stood there for a few seconds in stunned silence, transfixed, and then the church reappeared in its present state again.

Neither one of us was afraid of ghosts, so we were not really scared. Still, it was minutes before either of us could speak. Then Gus finally said, "Nobody is going to believe this!" I don't know about such things, but I think now that we had somehow gotten into a time warp for that brief instant. I have heard about such things. But how else can you explain what happened? All I know is that it was a once-in-a-lifetime experience that I will never forget.

PART IV
COLONIAL WILLIAMSBURG

"Mad Lucy" of Ludwell-Paradise House

Some called her (perhaps too generously) eccentric, capricious, whimsical or odd. Others said that she was just plain crazy. Whatever it was, it is certain that she was one of a kind, and her curious behavior caused excited titters of whispered gossip in the upper strata of eighteenth-century social circles on two continents. It is probable that had she not been from a well-to-do family, she might have been committed to a mental institution early in her life. As it was, her actions were covered up, embarrassingly laughed off or otherwise explained away as those of a high-strung young lady with a flair for being mischievous.

She was Lucy Ludwell, second daughter of Philip Ludwell III. She married John Paradise, a scholar and an accepted member of the intellectual set. Lucy lived much of her life in London and, according to one published account, "[s]tartled society by such exploits as dashing boiling water from her tea urn on a too garrulous gentleman who annoyed her."

Early in the eighteenth century, her grandfather had built a town residence in Williamsburg, Virginia, a handsome brick mansion. Surrounding the main house were stables, a paddock, a well, a smokehouse, a "necessary" house and a woodhouse close to the kitchen.

The Ludwell-Paradise House in Colonial Williamsburg was the home of "Mad Lucy" Ludwell, whose spirit is heard splashing in the bathtub two centuries after she died.

Property Lucy inherited in Virginia was confiscated by the commonwealth during the Revolutionary War because the politics espoused by her husband were alien to the cause of the colonists fighting for their freedom. In 1805, however, ten years after her husband died, Lucy set sail for America and was allowed to take up residence in what became known as the Ludwell-Paradise House.

It was here, as she got along in age, that she again became the talk of the town for her peculiar habits. For openers, Lucy, because of her social position in London, considered herself above her friends and neighbors in Virginia. She had a haughty attitude that she made no effort to disguise. One of Lucy's quirks was her penchant for borrowing the new clothes of her lady friends, especially hats. She viewed herself as a fashion plate of the times and seemed oblivious to the fact that everyone in town knew when she was donning loaned clothing. On Sundays, the congregation at her church always got a chuckle because Lucy regularly had her "little black boy," a servant's son, carry her prayer book into church ahead of her to announce her imminent entrance.

Lucy is perhaps best remembered for entertaining guests on weird carriage rides. They were weird in that they never went anywhere. She had a favorite coach reassembled on the back porch of her house. When callers dropped by, she would invite them into the coach and then have it rolled back and forth across the porch on imaginary trips by a servant. Her fantasy carriage rides became so frequent and her other eccentricities so pronounced that Lucy began having difficulty differentiating between the worlds of reality and make believe. Eventually, in 1812, she was committed to the state asylum for the insane in Williamsburg.

While Lucy died two years later, her spirit apparently remained attached to the Ludwell-Paradise House. A number of occupants over the years have reported hearing strange sounds there not attributable to any known physical source. Most notable of the witnesses are Mr. and Mrs. Rudolph Bares. He is a retired vice-president of Colonial Williamsburg who lived in the house for several years in the 1960s and 1970s:

Oh, we never heard any ghostly voices, saw any levitations or anything like that. But my wife and I each experienced the same odd phenomenon on several different occasions, maybe ten or twelve separate times. And that is, we would be downstairs when we would hear the water running in a second-floor bathtub. Then we would hear a splashing sound in the tub, as if someone was taking a bath. The first few times we heard it, we went up the stairs to take a look, but there was never anything or anyone there, and no water was running in the tub. So after a while, we wouldn't even check when we heard it. We'd just laugh and say it must be Lucy pouring a bath for herself.

Cleanliness, it should be noted, was another of Mad Lucy's idiosyncrasies. She was known to have taken as many as six baths a day!

THE PUZZLING RIDDLE OF THE "REFUSAL ROOM"

It has been described by many as the most beautiful house in America. Indeed, the stately Georgian mansion, shaded by a row of enormous old tulip poplar trees overlooking the scenic James River, remains a magnificent building even though it is more than 250 years old. Carter's Grove, in James City County near Williamsburg, Virginia, is rich in history.

Construction of the house began in 1750 on a 1,400-acre tract of land bought by the legendary colonist Robert "King" Carter, one of the wealthiest and most influential men of his time. The house and grounds today are privately owned, but for years up until early in the twenty-first century, they were open to the public; tens of thousands of tourists visited the plantation yearly, marveling at its majesty. For more than two hundred years, it was a showplace residence, and many lavish and memorable parties and dinners were held here for rich and famous personages.

Like other plantation homes along the James River, Carter's Grove also has its share of colorful legends and anecdotes. There are, for example, deep scars in the handsome, hand-hewn stair railing leading up from the front hall on the first floor. They were said to have been made during the Revolutionary War by the British cavalryman Colonel Banastre Tarleton, who rode his horse up the stairway, "hacking the balastrade with his saber as he ascended," according to a Colonial Williamsburg publication.

If ever there was a site ripe for the spiritual hauntings of unrestful souls, it well could be Carter's Grove; on the grounds is the spot at which a great tragedy occurred more than 350 years ago. Here, archaeologists searching for eighteenth-century artifacts surprisingly uncovered the remnants of a colony of early settlers dating to the year 1619. The settlement was known as Martin's Hundred, and all residents of it were massacred by Indians in 1622.

The "Refusal Room" in Carter's Grove, near Williamsburg, is where two young ladies allegedly turned down marriage proposals from George Washington and Thomas Jefferson. According to legend, one of the ladies returns in spirit form to tear up carnation petals and scatter them about the room.

Through the years, there have been strange occurrences at the plantation that tend to support the belief that paranormal phenomena is involved. There is, for instance, the story told by husband and wife caretakers, who were alone at the estate one evening. While doing chores in different parts of the west end of the mansion, each distinctly heard footsteps coming from the east end. The man assumed it was his wife and vice versa. Later, when they met, each learned that the other had not ventured into the east end of the house. A search revealed no cause for the sounds. A former supervisor of tour guides told of an old gardener who occasionally heard a woman playing a harp in an upstairs bedroom. No one could ever convince him otherwise, although no known source for the musical interludes was ever found.

It is in a downstairs drawing room, however, that the most celebrated ghost of Carter's Grove apparently resides. Longtime servants at the mansion were convinced that this room was haunted. It was here that a pretty young woman, Mary Cary, allegedly turned down a proposal for marriage in the mid-eighteenth century from an ardent suitor—George Washington! Some years later, in the same room, Thomas Jefferson offered his hand to the fair Rebecca Burwell. He, too, was rejected. This parlor subsequently became known as the "Refusal Room."

In the years since, some peculiar things kept reoccurring in the room. Most notably, whenever white carnations were placed in it, they were mysteriously ripped to shreds late at night by unseen hands and scattered about. No one knows who did it or why only white carnations were affected—and only the ones in the Refusal Room, whereas other flowers in the house remained untouched.

In 1939, the Associated Press carried a nationwide article on the phenomenon, quoting Mrs. Archibald McCrea, then owner of the house. She said at the time that it was true that "something" was coming in at night to "blight her blooms." Traps were set for mice, but they were never sprung. John Coleman, an elderly butler, said it was "ghosts!"

When the plantation was open to the public, tour hostesses said that they, too, occasionally found the shredded petals of white carnations littered about the room. No one at the site, present or past, has offered any semblance of a rational explanation for such apparent supernatural activity. It was highly doubtful that the torn flowers were the work of a prankster, because when the house was open, tour guides were always in or near the room, and when the house was closed at night, security guards kept a close watch; there were also alarm systems throughout that would have been triggered by anyone prowling about.

Could it be the spirit of one of the two famous spurned lovers, unable to control his emotion at being rejected? Possibly. But some believe that it may be the spectral return of one of the young women who refused. It is said that when Mary Cary watched the triumphant Continental army enter the area after the Yorktown surrender at the end of the Revolutionary War in 1781, commanded by General George Washington, she was so overcome by chagrin that she fainted away in her husband's arms.

So it is speculated that it may be her spirit that sometimes slipped into the house late at night to tear the carnations in a fit of anger at what might have been had she accepted Washington's original bouquet of flowers and proposal offer so long ago.

PART V
RIVER AREAS

THE RAPPING FRIEND OF THE OYSTERMEN

At Fort Eustis, near Newport News, Virginia, there is a small, sheltered cove where the waters of Nell's Creek feed into the historic James River. Decades ago, before the government purchased the land surrounding this area, Nell's Creek was a haven for Tidewater oystermen. Daily they would ply their time-honored trade amid the rich oyster beds of the river, and at night some would stay in the mouth of the creek from Monday until Friday, when they would take their catch to market and head home.

According to local lore, this particular creek was named after a young lady named Nell, who lived in the region during the nineteenth century. What has been passed down is that she was a spirited, headstrong person who fell in love with a man described as a straggler and that her father strongly objected to such a union. In fact, he allegedly told her that if she violated his wishes and married the man, he would kill her and bury her along with all of his money.

Despite his warning, she supposedly ran off with her lover, and her father lived up to his threat. He killed her and buried her, along with his life savings, at a point on or near the creek beneath two large walnut trees. Since that time, no one is exactly sure when it all began, although the prevailing opinion is that from about the 1880s or 1890s up until the 1930s, the spirit of Nell reappeared, mostly through the psychic manifestation of knockings or rappings, to area oystermen. She apparently was a friendly ghost who provided timely news on where the best oyster hunting was from day to day, and she often played games in which she seemed to enjoy answering questions, mostly concerning numbers and figures. Why she chose to befriend the lonely watermen is a question that remains unanswered.

The story was best told by a seventy-nine-year-old former oysterman known as "J.P.," who doesn't want his real name used for fear of being mocked. For many years in the 1920s and 1930s, J.P. worked the waters of the James with his father and brother.

"I definitely believe she was there. There's no doubt in my mind," he says of Nell. "I'm not a superstitious person, but in this instance I do believe. I only experienced her presence once, but it was something I will never forget. My father and brother heard her many times, and they believed. And they wouldn't tell a lie for anything. Many say it was all a myth, but a lot of people swear they heard her." As J.P. told it, the stories about Nell began surfacing late in the nineteenth century. No one ever saw her. They heard her. She "appeared" by knocking on the cabin roofs of the oystermen's boats.

"It was a knock unlike any other I have ever heard," J.P. recalls. "It was different. I can't even describe it. I guess I was about eighteen or twenty when I experienced it. We were laid up overnight in the cove, and I was standing outside the cabin with my head tucked inside, listening to the conversation. The cabin was full of watermen, talking. There was a very distinct knocking on the top of the cabin. When I poked my head outside, it sounded like it came from the inside, and when I ducked my head inside the cabin, it was like it came from the outside. There was no way it could have been a trick or hoax. I wasn't really scared, but I must have looked concerned, because someone laughed and said, 'That's just ole Nell.'"

J.P. says that his father told him many times about the rappings. "He would never volunteer to talk about her, but if you asked, he would tell you." What J.P.'s father said was that she "talked" through her rappings. One rap meant yes and two meant no. "In those days, people oystered over many sites up and down the river," J.P. says. "Some would come out of the Warwick River, Deep Creek, Squashers Hole and other places. Every rock in the river had a name, and the men knew them all. So they would ask Nell how their peers were doing at other locations. Like, they would ask how many bushels of oysters did they get today at Thomas rock, near the James River bridge. And Nell would give so many knocks."

If the harvests were better elsewhere, according to J.P., then those asking the questions of Nell would fish those waters the next day. Invariably, their hauls improved. "Only a few of the men took stock in this," J.P. acknowledged, "but those who did always benefited from the advice. And she was always right. If she said so many bushels were brought in at such and such a rock, it was so."

Nell amazed the men with all sorts of revelations. "She could answer anything she was asked," J.P. said. "You could ask her how many children someone had, and she would rap out the number in knocks on the cabin. You could ask her someone's age, and she knew it exactly. My father said one time a man grabbed a handful of beans out of a sack and asked her how many he had. She told him, to the bean!" In this manner, Nell carried on conversations with a number of oystermen over the years. She was especially conversant with one man, J.P. noted, "and it was told that when he died she even appeared at his funeral by rapping on his coffin."

Robert Forrest, a lifelong native of the area, well remembers his ancestors talking about Nell. "Oh, yes," he said, "I've heard the tales. The one I remember best concerned an old man named John who was a very religious fellow. He had heard about Nell, too, and he didn't believe the stories until the night he experienced the sensation himself. He went out with some oystermen one time just to prove there was nothing to the legend. He carried his Bible with him.

"Well," Forrest continued, "they laid up in the Deep Creek area that night and tried to rouse her. 'Nell,' they said, 'if you're here, rap twice on the cabin.' Nothing happened. About thirty minutes later, they tried again, and sure enough, this time there were two sharp raps. They asked her several questions, and she responded to each of them, but John still wasn't convinced. He thought someone was playing a trick on him, so he went out on deck. There was no one there and no boats nearby. Not only that, but the boat John was on had also been untied from its stakes and was drifting freely in the creek. John became a believer right there!"

J.P. says that his brother was reading the Bible to Nell one night, the chapter of Deuteronomy, when the knockings on the cabin became louder and louder and got out of control. He stopped reading, and she stopped. "He never read the Bible to her again." Deuteronomy, it may be remembered, includes the ten commandments, among which are "Thou shalt not kill" and "Honor thy father." "No wonder Nell was disturbed," said J.P. "All she ever told us was that her father had killed her and buried her nearby with his money. So one time my father and brother went off digging in a spot where there were two large walnut trees. Except the whole time they were there, they were pestered by large swarms of hornets or wasps, and they had to give it up."

Randolph Rollins, a retired Poquoson carpenter, told of others who went looking for the lost loot. "One time they were driven off by a cloud of bees. They took that as an omen. Another time, a sudden storm whipped up and the wind nearly took down one of the trees. That scared them off and they never came back." J.P., however, was not discouraged by all that. He was one who thought that there really was money buried somewhere in the Nell's Creek vicinity. "If I could, I would have spent every penny I had to buy some land there," he said, "but, of course, you couldn't. The government owns it. I sure wish I could talk to ole Nell again. I've tried many times, but she's never answered."

In fact, no one has heard from Nell for more than seventy years. She was a friend of the oystermen for half a century or so, but when the military took over Fort Eustis, the knockings ceased. "She must be at peace now," J.P. surmised.

THE REVENGE OF "DOLLY MAMMY"

There is a striking similarity between the infamous Bell Witch of Tennessee and the ghost of "Dolly Mammy" Messick, who surfaced several decades later in the town of Poquoson, Virginia. The Bell Witch allegedly returned from death to taunt a family who had cheated her in life. A specific target was a teenage girl named Betsy Bell.

Poquoson is located on a plat of land between Seaford and Yorktown to the north and west and just above Hampton to the south and east. It derives its colorful name from the Algonquin Indian word *pocosin*, which means a swamp or dismal place. It is nearly surrounded by water and is adjacent to the Plum Tree National Wildlife Refuge. Since colonial times, Poquoson has been the home of rugged and closely knit clans of watermen and farmers. Many current families can date their ancestors in the area back hundreds of years.

For generations, area residents owning cattle let their animals roam freely in lush, marshy regions known locally as "the Commons." Such was the case with "Dolly Mammy" Messick, a no-nonsense, hardworking and well-liked woman whose tragic story and haunting reappearances have been remembered and recounted from generation to generation.

There is some confusion as to when she died. Some believe it was in the 1850s. And yet, according to Bill Forrest, a local resident who says that Dolly was his great-great-aunt, there is a mention in the *Poquoson Waterman* book, an unofficial genealogical guide, that states that she passed away in 1904 at age forty-two.

Whatever the case, it is agreed that it was a cold, blustery day laden with dark, heavy clouds hovering over the lowlands. Fearing a storm, Dolly decided to go out into the marshlands to bring in her cows and asked her teenage daughters, Minnie and Lettie Jane, to help her. Ensconced comfortably before a fire in the farmhouse, the girls sassed their mother and steadfastly refused.

Angrily flinging on a cloak, Dolly turned to her daughters and warned that if anything happened to her she would return to "hant" them for the rest of their lives. With that, she disappeared into the gloom. When she had not come back by dark, a search party of friends and neighbors was hastily organized, and they tramped through the swamps with lanterns, calling her name, but they found nothing.

The next morning, a lone fisherman, easing his boat up Bell's Oyster Gut, a narrow estuary near the Messick home, was startled at the sight of a bare human leg sticking up out of the marsh grasses. He went for help, and soon the body of Dolly Mammy was recovered. She apparently had been sucked into a pocket of quicksand. It appeared that she had desperately struggled for her life, because the rushes and grasses around her body had been pulled up. Her funeral was well attended.

Not long after that, the haunting threat of Dolly Mammy began to be carried out. One day, her daughters went to visit nearby relations. No sooner had they arrived when ghostly knockings began to echo loudly throughout the house. Suspecting pranksters, a family member grabbed a heavy piece of wood and barred the door. Incredibly, the bar leaped into the air from its iron fastenings and flew across the room. The knockings, described as sounding like an iron fist beating on a thin board, continued and grew in intensity so much that they were heard a quarter of a mile away. The girls cowered in fear.

While the thunderous knockings—which seemed to follow the girls wherever they went—continued as the main form of spectral manifestation, there were many other strange incidents as well. "All sorts of things started to happen," says Randolph Rollins, a lifelong resident of Poquoson. His grandfather was a witness to some of the events.

"I can remember him telling me about one night the two girls slept together in a bed, and the next morning when they woke up their hair was tightly braided together," he says. "No one could ever explain that." As the months passed, relatives and neighbors spent considerable time at Dolly's house trying to console the distraught daughters. Rollins's grandfather was one of them.

"He told me many a time about being in the house when a table in the middle of the living room with a lamp on it would start shaking and jumping up and down. Then the lamp would go out, and it would be dark, and he could hear the sounds of someone being slapped. When he relit the lamp, the girls would have red marks on their faces with the imprint of a hand. He said this happened a number of times," Rollins recalls. Once, witnesses claimed, as the girls lay in deep sleep in their bed, something lifted the bed off the floor and shook it violently. Another time, an unseen hand snatched a Bible from beneath the pillow of one of the girls and flung it against a wall.

As in the much documented case of the Bell Witch of Tennessee, as word of the eerie manifestations circulated, curiosity seekers from all over came to the house. An army officer from nearby Fort Monroe arrived with the intention of debunking the ghost as a myth. He had his men search the house from cellar to attic and then had guards surround it to ward off any tricksters. Yet that evening, as he sat in the parlor, the knockings were so loud that they could be heard half a mile away. Then a lamp seemed to lift itself from a table, sailed through the room and landed on the mantel. Having seen and heard enough, the bewildered officer wrote in a report, "Whatever causes the disturbances is of a supernatural nature."

Rollins says that once when his grandfather was in the house, two skeptical lawyers showed up. The rappings were so deafening that normal conversation couldn't be heard, and they abruptly fled. And one memorable evening, a spirit medium was invited to hold a séance in the house. It was attended by the girls and a large group of people. According to published accounts of the affair, a "shadowy figure" appeared, winding a ball of yarn. As the figure responded to various commands of the medium, the girls fainted.

Then the medium said, "If you are the mother of these girls and are connected with these rappings [which were going on simultaneously], speak." The girls' names were then called out, followed by wild, shrieking laughter. That was enough to clear the room. This single "appearance" seemed to be the high point of the hauntings. When one of the daughters died, the knockings and other phenomena ceased. The mother had made good on her threat.

There is a brief epilogue. In the lush marshes and thick grass of the Commons, through which Poquoson cows once roamed freely, there is one small patch of land on which, curiously, no vegetation has grown since early this century. It is precisely the spot where the body of Dolly Mammy had been found.

THE CELEBRITY SPIRITS OF FORT MONROE

There are so many ghosts, famous or otherwise, at historic Fort Monroe in Hampton, Virginia, that it's hard to know where to begin. One can almost take his or her pick of a celebrity specter, and chances are that "it" has been sighted at some point over the past two centuries. The star-studded list of apparitions that allegedly have appeared at one time or another include Abraham Lincoln; Jefferson Davis and his wife, Varina; General Ulysses S. Grant; the Marquis de Lafayette; Indian chief Black Hawk; and a budding young author and poet named Edgar Allan Poe. In fact, the only notable

These quarters at historic Fort Monroe, near Hampton, once housed a young lieutenant named Robert E. Lee. A number of sites at the fort are believed to be haunted.

who either served or visited the fort and has not returned in spirit form is Robert E. Lee, who as a young lieutenant helped with the engineering and construction of the facility in the 1830s.

The list of haunts at Fort Monroe is not limited to the well known, however. There also are numerous nameless ones, including illicit lovers and a bevy of perky poltergeists that have been accused of such indignities as smacking officers in the face with flying dish towels and tossing heavy, marble-laden tables across rooms. There are even reports, serious ones, of a reptilian monster that has been seen stirring in the ancient moat that surrounds the fort.

Dennis Mroczkowski, former director of the Casemate Museum in Hampton, offers a thought about why so many spirits seem to frequent the site. "With the hundreds of thousands of people who have been assigned to the fort," he says, "there's a large population to draw from for ghosts. There have been multiple sightings of strange apparitions, and many tend to repeat themselves and become identified in people's minds with the famous men who have been here." He also believes that the dank and dreary corridors and the thick-walled casemates possibly could have lent inspiration to the later macabre writings of onetime resident Poe.

The history of the area dates back to the time of the first English settlement in America. The hardy souls aboard the *Godspeed, Susan Constant* and *Discovery* saw Old Point Comfort (where Fort Monroe is located) in April 1607, at least two weeks before they dropped anchor at Jamestown. A small exploration party even rowed ashore and met with local Indians.

In 1608, Captain John Smith checked the area out and deemed it an excellent site for a fort. Consequently, a year later, Captain John Ratcliffe was dispatched from Jamestown to build an earthwork fortification that was called Fort Algernourne. By 1611, it was well stockaded and had a battery of seven heavy guns and a garrison of forty men. A century later, there were seventy cannons at the fort, and in 1728, a new brick facility was constructed at Old Point Comfort and was renamed Fort George. This structure was completely destroyed by a fierce hurricane in 1749.

The strategic military value of the site was recognized by the French under Admiral Comte de Grasse during the Revolutionary War when his men reerected a battery here. The War of 1812 demonstrated the need for an adequate American coastal defense, and over the next few years plans were drawn up for an elaborate system of forts running from Maine to Louisiana. Old Point Comfort was selected as a key post in this chain, and the assignment for building a new fort here was given to Brigadier General Simon Bernard, a famous French military engineer and former aide-decamp to Emperor Napoleon I. Construction extended over fifteen years, from 1819 to 1834, and it was named Fort Monroe after James Monroe, a Virginian and the fifth president of the United States.

Upon its completion, the fort had an armament of nearly two hundred guns, which controlled the channel into Hampton Roads and dominated the approach to Washington by way of the Chesapeake Bay. So impregnable was this bastion, and so ideally located, it was one of the few Union fortifications in the South that was not captured by the Confederates during the Civil War. It was described as an unassailable base for the Union army and navy, right in the heart of the Confederacy. Thus President Abraham Lincoln had no qualms about visiting the fort in May 1862 to help plan the attack of Norfolk. It was here, too, where General U.S. Grant outlined the campaign strategy that led to the end of the Civil War.

And many believe it was also at Fort Monroe, a year later, that the imprisonment of Jefferson Davis, the president of the Confederate States of America, led to one of the first and most famous ghost stories associated with the site. Davis, who had been planning to reestablish the capital of the Confederacy in Texas with hopes of continuing the war, was captured near Irwinville, Georgia, on May 10, 1865. His devoted wife, Varina, rushed forward when it appeared that a Northern cavalryman was about to shoot down her defiant husband, who also had been accused, inaccurately, of plotting an attempt to assassinate President Lincoln.

Davis was taken to Fort Monroe, then the most powerful fort in the country, to prevent escape or rescue attempts. On May 23, 1865, he was placed in solitary confinement in a cell in Casemate No. 2, a stone-walled chamber, creating a painful incident that almost cost him his life and may well have provided the cause for the periodic spectral return of Varina Davis to Fort Monroe.

A day after his imprisonment, Davis was ordered to be shackled. When a blacksmith knelt down to rivet the ankle irons in place, the angered Davis knocked him to the floor. He sprang to his feet, raised his hammer and was about to crush the Southerner's skull when the officer of the day, Captain Jerome Titlow, threw himself between the two men. Thereafter, it took four Union soldiers to subdue Davis long enough for the irons to be secured.

The next day, Dr. John J. Craven, chief medical officer at the fort, examined the prisoner and was shocked at his sickly appearance. He quickly recommended that the shackles be removed, and they were a few days later. Meanwhile, the determined Varina fought hard for more humane treatment of her husband, and eventually she and Dr. Craven were successful. Davis was moved to better quarters in Carroll Hall. In May 1866, Varina got permission from President Andrew Johnson to join Davis at the fort, and she brought along their young daughter, Winnie. Davis was released from captivity on May 13, 1867, traveled extensively in Europe and later retired to Beauvoir, a mansion in Biloxi, Mississippi. He died in 1889 at the age of eighty-one and today is buried in Hollywood Cemetery in Richmond, Virginia.

It is supposedly the apparition of the iron-willed Varina that has been seen on occasion at the fort, appearing late at night through the second-floor window of quarters located directly across from the casemate where her husband had been harshly shackled. A number of residents have reported seeing her. One awoke early one morning to glimpse the figures of both "a plumpish woman and a young girl peering through the window." The witness got out of bed and walked toward them, but when she reached out to touch to woman's billowing skirt, the figures disappeared.

Varied Spectral Activity

A wide range of psychic phenomena has been experienced in a splendid old plantation-style house facing the east sally port that is known as Old Quarters No. 1. Manifestations have included the clumping of boots, the rustling of silken skirts, the sounds of distant laughter and the strange shredding of fresh flower petals in midwinter. It is here, appropriately enough in the Lincoln Room, where the image of Honest Abe himself has been seen clad in a dressing gown and standing by the fireplace, appearing to be deep in thought. According to Jane Keane Polonsky and Jean McFarland Drum, who in 1972 published a book on the ghosts of Fort Monroe, other residents of this house have told of seeing Lafayette, Grant and Chief Black Hawk wandering about. All of them stayed at Old Quarters No. 1 during their lifetimes.

"Ghost Alley," a lane that runs behind a set of quarters long known as the "Tuileries," is the setting for one of the oldest and saddest legends of the supernatural at Fort Monroe. It is here, always under the cloak of darkness, that the fabled "White Lady" has been seen searching for her long-lost lover. In the versions that have been handed down for a century and a half, she was a beautiful young woman who once lived in a Tuileries unit with a much older husband, a captain, who has been described as stodgy and plodding.

Being of a flirtatious nature, she inevitably (and, as it turned out, tragically) attracted the attentions of a dashing younger officer, and their obvious longings for each other soon became apparent to all but the unimaginative captain. And when he left on a trip, the young lovers consummated their relationship. The captain, however, returned unexpectedly early one evening and caught the lovers. In a fit of rage, he shot and killed his wife. Ever since, she has been sighted fleetingly in a luminescent form roaming the dark alley looking for her handsome companion in hopes of rekindling their once fervent romance.

Undoubtedly, the most famous enlisted man ever to serve at Fort Monroe, even if it was only for a few brief months, was nineteen-year-old Edgar Allan Poe. He arrived at the fort on December 15, 1828, and almost immediately sought help to get out of the army so he could pursue a career in writing. He was successful and was discharged at Fort Monroe on April 15, 1829. He is known to have returned to the area once, twenty years later, when he recited some poetry at the old Hygeia Hotel on September 9, 1849, just four weeks before his death in Baltimore.

It is the spectral image of Poe, many have speculated, that was seen during the late 1960s at housing quarters on Bernard Road, which, by coincidence, backs onto Ghost Alley. It was here where a lady tenant of the house heard a mysterious tapping coming from the rear of a downstairs room one night in May 1968. Upon investigation, she saw the figure of a man dressed in a white shirt with puffed sleeves, a red vest and dark pants. She couldn't see his face in the shadows, even as he turned to give her a disdainful look. In an instant, he vanished in a gray mist through a window. Oddly, it was the same window through which the woman's son, a year earlier, had reported seeing a white mist float toward him and then vaporize. The shadowy figure was sighted once more in 1969, in a bent-over, crouching position, moving down a hallway, where it was said to have gone through a closet door without opening the door!

Poltergeists!

In other parts of Fort Monroe, playful and noisy ghosts have both frightened and amused but most often bewildered residents. At the Old Slave Quarters, for example, officers, their wives and children have been subjected to a series of strange shenanigans over the years. Several tenants have found their downstairs furniture rearranged or shoved into the middle of the room overnight, with no rational explanation for how or why it was done. One couple locked their pet cat in the kitchen one night in hopes that it would rid the room of mice. Inexplicably, they found the cat outside at the back door the next day, meowing to get back in.

At a two-story house next to the chapel, occupants found that a heavy chest had been moved during the night and fireplace andirons rearranged. On other occasions, footsteps heard at night ceased each time a light was turned on, drawers seemed to be opened and shut by unseen hands, doors slammed and loud bangings and hammerings occurred. Even the post commander's quarters has been affected. There, such items as a pedestal cake stand and a Dresden figurine have been discovered broken overnight, with no apparent cause.

The stories do abound at Fort Monroe. There is even an instance of a colonel who told of sighting a "monster" swimming about in the moat that encircles the fort. It was reported to be 60 to 150 feet wide and 8 feet deep at high tide. The colonel said that whatever he saw was pretty big. He followed it to an old footbridge, where it disappeared.

The thing about all of these happenings at the fort, aside from the sheer number of them, is the consistency with which they have been told and retold over the years, in most cases by more than one person and in some instances by many. The other thing is the durability of the incidents. Some are alleged to have occurred decades or even a century or more ago. Others are much more recent. The ghostly encounters continue to this day.

Workers at the Casemate Museum tell of the relatively recent visit of an obviously shaken wife of an officer. She had heard of the many paranormal tales at the fort and wanted to share her own unnerving experience. She said that she had been in a bedroom with her two teenagers watching television one night, while her husband was in the basement. Before their startled eyes, a bedside table lifted up and flew across the room, smashing into the fireplace and shattering the marble top. She and her children screamed, and their dog went wild, pawing at the floor. Oddly, a Waterford crystal lamp that had been on the table remained unscratched.

And finally, there was the officer and his wife who were living in the quarters where Robert E. Lee was once housed. The husband was in the kitchen one night when a wet dishcloth sailed across the room and smacked him soundly in the face. He yelled at his wife, asking her why she had done that. She didn't answer. He discovered later that she was outside the house at the time.

The playful poltergeists at Fort Monroe apparently were at it again!

THE GHOST SOLDIER OF NELSON HOUSE

Had not fate intervened, chances are that relatively few Americans would ever have heard of the sleepy, peaceful little village of Yorktown, Virginia, located about fifteen miles northeast of Williamsburg. Destiny, however, stepped in more than two hundred years ago and indelibly inscribed it as a prominent name in American history. It was here, during a few days in October 1781, where General George Washington, commander of the American armies, outmaneuvered General George Cornwallis and defeated his once proud British forces during a furious siege that, for all practical purposes, ended the Revolutionary War.

Today, Yorktown remains a relatively quiet little community, its peacefulness interrupted each summer by thousands of tourists who walk the hallowed battlegrounds on which America's independence was courageously secured. One of the most imposing landmarks here is a large brick house perched on a hill overlooking the York River. The personal history of the Nelson House is inexorably intertwined with the growing pangs of a young nation struggling for its freedom. It also played a dramatic part in the final battle at Yorktown, and therein lies a ghostly legend that has survived the centuries. The house is allegedly haunted by the spirit of a British soldier who was killed in the final fighting in 1781 by an ironic twist of luck.

A massive structure of red brick, with stone trim and ivy-covered walls, Nelson House dates to the early 1700s and has been called one of the best examples of Georgian architecture in Virginia. It was built by the ancestors of Thomas Nelson, a member of the Continental Congress, commanding general of the Virginia militia, a governor of Virginia and a signer of the Declaration of Independence. In the years preceding the war, Thomas Nelson and his bride, the former Lucy Grymes of Brandon, entertained all of the great dignitaries of the colony here. The family had to abandon the house when the British occupied the town.

On the morning of October 9, 1781, General George Washington's men and their allied forces, including artillery, were strategically set in place to commence the final battle. The bombardment began about 3:00 p.m. General Nelson was asked to single out a good target toward which the cannon crews could direct their fire. Stoically, and without hesitation, he pointed to a large brick mansion on a hill, which he suggested might be serving as Cornwallis's headquarters. The house Nelson indicated was his own!

Cannon fire was directed toward it, and several shells directly hit the target. One apparently penetrated a secret stairway hidden behind a panel

The Thomas Nelson House in Yorktown became famous during the last days of the Revolutionary War, when Nelson told George Washington to direct his cannon fire at Nelson's own house. One of the shells is believed to have killed a British soldier hiding there, and his ghost occasionally makes its presence known.

in the dining room hall leading to a garret. According to the legend, it was here where a British soldier was hiding. He was killed by the blast, and it is his ghost that remains a sad and restless presence.

The house remained in the Nelson family until 1907. A few years later, it was purchased by Captain George Preston Blow. The Blows entertained here in a manner reminiscent of the way the Nelsons had done so many years earlier. It was during one of these socials that the ghost made its most noted showing. Mrs. Blow was hosting a luncheon for several ladies. One of the guests asked her if the house was haunted. Mrs. Blow said, "Goodness, no."

Apparently, this infuriated the spirit, because, according to eyewitness accounts, no sooner had she spoken than the secret door behind the panel in the dining room suddenly burst open with such terrific force that it shook the entire house and knocked against a sideboard with such violence that dishes crashed to the floor. There was a stony silence in the room, save for the muffled gasps of the obviously terrified guests. Finally, Mrs. Blow managed to say that the incident had been caused by a sudden downdraft of air. No one believed her. Fearful of a further display of psychic power, the ladies abruptly departed.

In 1968, Nelson House was acquired by the National Park Service and is open to the public. To this day, however, tour guides, when asked about the ghost, are unusually careful about their comments.

The Phantom Mourners

Thomas Nelson is buried in the little cemetery adjacent to Yorktown's historic Grace Episcopal Church, built in 1697. Thousands of tourists visit this sacred site annually. Those who venture inside the building may happen upon a ghost. The figure of a woman, dressed in eighteenth-century clothing, has been seen by a number of witnesses over the years. She appears to be crying, her head buried in prayer. Some say that she is holding a lifeless child. Her identity and purpose have never been discovered.

There also are occasional sightings, dating back more than two centuries, of a spectral band of mourners in the graveyard, apparently gathered for a funeral. In 1791, Samuel Hawkins wrote in his journal:

> *As I walked past the old church yesterday morning, I witnessed the burial ceremony of a beloved citizen. I was uncertain of who it was, but the people in attendance were indeed upset over his passing. One of the women beside the grave fell to her knees with grief.*
>
> *I thought it proper to offer my condolences, so I approached the grave site. It was then I saw the mournful group, draped in black costumes, dissolve into thin air! I now realize that I witnessed a funeral from days gone by.*

Others have told of seeing the same phenomenon. In recent years, a resident jogging by the church one day said, "I saw a group of people gathered around one of the graves. I stopped to watch. The women wore black skirts that dragged to the ground, and the men wore pants which ended at the knee, with stockings that went from their knees to their feet. The men had shoes with buckles, and some had capes thrown around their necks... Something just wasn't right with the scene."

PART VI
PORTSMOUTH/NORFOLK AREA

LEGENDS OF THE GREAT DISMAL SWAMP

Whoever named the Great Dismal Swamp knew exactly what he was doing. For the past four centuries, it has been described by those who have been there, both the famous and the infamous, in the darkest and most brooding terms. Colonel William Byrd II, dispatched there to help designate the line dividing Virginia and North Carolina in the seventeenth century, wrote: "It is a horrible desert, with foul damps ascending without ceasing, corrupting the air, and rendering it unfit for respiration...having vapours which infest the air and causing ague and other distempers to the neighboring inhabitants. Toward the center of it no beast or bird approaches, nor so much as an insect or reptile exists. Not even a turkey buzzard will venture to fly over it."

Authors have painted the Great Dismal Swamp as alluring, capricious and contradictory. One wrote of the area that "[l]ike a beautiful woman, she tantalizes with her oft changing moods. She encourages recklessness, but metes out swift and cruel punishment to those whom she lures into her web of dangers. She sadistically sears their souls with wounds which never heal; wounds which forever must be soothed through distorted imaginations, tall tales, and uncontrolled enthusiasm for anything pertaining to the swamp."

Legends of the Great Dismal Swamp in extreme southeastern Virginia include a wide variety of unexplained paranormal activity.

Another writer has said that Great Dismal was "an almost impenetrable wilderness, a treacherous bog, refuge of deadly snakes and every kind of wildlife. Here fled the wanted men and runaway slaves and those who would abandon the company of men. Many were never heard of again for the grim wilderness seldom gave of its secrets."

There are indeed common tales of huge eastern black bears attacking human victims, cracking their skulls with a single swipe from their massive paws. Many people firmly believe that there are bats in the quagmire that suck people's blood. In colonial days, Great Dismal teemed with wildlife. As one journalist put it: "Its tangled Juniper and canebrake were hung with snakes, and serpents fell without a warning hiss out of trees onto boats."

Today, Great Dismal Swamp is a 120,000-acre reserve, about forty miles long and fifteen miles wide, on the Virginia–North Carolina line, which borders the cities of Suffolk and Chesapeake along its northern limits. At its heart is huge Lake Drummond, named for a colonial governor of North Carolina who discovered it while hunting.

Colorful legends of the swamp have been passed down for nearly four hundred years and have not only endured but thrived. Many originated with the Indians who once roamed here. Some told of "firebirds" abducting

Lake Drummond, in the midst of the Great Dismal Swamp in southeastern Virginia, has been the scene of a variety of psychic phenomena.

Indian maidens and of great battles by famous warriors to overcome these supernatural beings. Other tales undoubtedly were spawned by the many slaves and fugitives from justice who sought refuge in the swamp and by the hermits, recluses and eccentrics who have lived deep in the forest interiors. Also, countless thousands of hunters who come to the region each season have unquestionably embellished such stories and added their own as they cooked dinner around their campfires on dark nights.

The swamp is supposedly inhabited by spirits, witches, dragons, ghouls and ghosts. There are weird sights of bizarre and mysterious lights in the dense jungles and around Lake Drummond, and all sorts of eerie sounds are heard at night throughout the swamp.

Here is a small sampling of some of the better-known legends that have survived the test of time.

The Fishing Bride

Captain Bill Crockett, a onetime merchant mariner who settled in Great Dismal Swamp after World War I, first as a lumberman and later as a hunting guide, often told the story of a beautiful maiden who lived at the edge of the swamp near Washington's Ditch. On the morning of her wedding day, her fiancé, a fearless lumberjack, set off into the forest to kill a deer for the reception feast.

When he didn't return at the wedding hour, the maiden assured the guests that he would be back, and as they continued partying, she slipped off into the swamp in her wedding gown to search for him. Neither was ever seen again.

Over the intervening years, numerous hunters and others have claimed to have seen a mysterious apparition on the south side of Lake Drummond. In the early morning, as the first pale shafts of light dart through the trees, a transparent beautiful maiden, resplendent in a white wedding gown, appears in the misty dawn and "glides" out onto a log several feet into the water, where she calmly baits her hook and casts her line out to catch a fresh fish for her lover's breakfast.

The Ghosts that Speak French

There are several accounts about an ill-fated French treasure ship that allegedly was blown off course during a voyage in the seventeenth century.

Chased by a British warship, the French vessel sought refuge in the Chesapeake Bay and then was followed up the Elizabeth River, where it ran aground in the mouth of Deep Creek.

Laden with a plundered cargo of Dutch and Spanish gold coins, the French sailors abandoned ship, hauling as much loot as they could carry, and headed into Great Dismal Swamp. They buried their treasure near the entrance, a theory strengthened by the fact that several caches of coins have been recovered there over the years. Soon after this, however, the pursuing English seamen caught up with them and killed them.

Since then, many swamp natives, hunters and visitors have reported hearing echoes of voices speaking in French near the entrance. The voices have been described as "having no earthly habitation." The general belief is that they belong to the slain French sailors, who return to the swamp to eternally guard the remainder of their gold.

The Strange Death of Black Jack, the Hermit

Snow blanketed the swamp one Christmas Eve shortly after the turn of the twentieth century, cloaking the trees and vines in a pure white shroud. Late in the afternoon, a hermit who lived at the edge of the forest and was known only as "Black Jack" set out in his small boat with his faithful hunting dog, rowed across Lake Drummond and then went down Washington Ditch a few miles. Near White Marsh Road, they landed and walked into the thick woods in search of a deer for dinner.

The dog flushed the largest white buck Jack had ever seen. White deer are legendary in the swamp. Indians say that they are protected by "the spirits." Perhaps so, because the buck froze in its tracks within a few feet of Jack, and he fired at near point-blank range. However, the deer didn't even flinch. It turned and romped freely into the woods, and the dog immediately lost its trail. Jack was shaken.

Some time later, the dog chased a huge red buck, and this time the hunter's shot rang true. By the time he got the deer into the boat and started home, it was almost dark. As he approached the center of the lake, a blue-green halo of light appeared in the sky just above the treetops. It first seemed to be the moon rising, but then the light moved rapidly toward the boat and hovered directly overhead, illuminating the whole lake like a giant spotlight. The grizzled old hermit was terribly frightened, and he rowed quickly to shore.

A ghostly tree guards the edge of the Great Dismal Swamp's haunted Lake Drummond.

He carried the heavy buck to his cabin, dropped it outside the door and ordered his dog to stand watch while he prepared to clean and dress it. Inside, he started a fire, got out of his cold, wet clothes and sharpened his knife. When he opened the door, both the dog and the deer were gone. Odd, because the dog would have barked at any disturbance. The hermit got his lantern and began a search. He found small patches of blood in a snow trail that led back to the lake's edge, where he had tied his boat. It appeared that the dog and the dead deer had entered the lake. Jack was stunned.

As he stood there, trying to figure things out, he heard a low moan. It grew louder and seemed to be coming from the center of the lake. As he looked out, the eerie blue-green halo of light seemed to rise out of the water and soar gracefully through the air to a spot just above a giant cypress. It increased in brightness and lit the tree with its glow.

Jack stood entranced by the spectacle. His hypnotic state was finally broken by the bloodcurdling scream of a wildcat. Shivering in the cold, Jack jumped into his boat, rowed across the lake, entered the feeder ditch and raced downstream to the locks. He tied up his boat and took the trail down the south side of the canal at Arbuckle's Landing, where he ran to Captain Crockett's cottage. He arrived at midnight, so cold and frightened that he wasn't able to talk for three hours. Finally, after being warmed by the fire and a liquid mixture of honey, swamp water and moonshine, he blurted out the story of what had happened.

Jack left the next morning in search of his lost dog and the missing deer. That night, Captain Crockett dreamed of the mysterious white deer and the halo of light. It came to him as a premonition that Jack was in danger, so the next morning he went to check on his friend. At the hermit's cabin, he found the door open and the fire out. He then hurried to the edge of the lake, where Jack kept his boat. There, he saw some tracks. He traced them into the thicket, and there he found Jack, in a kneeling position, frozen to death! There were no signs of a struggle and no other tracks.

Captain Crockett said that since that time, on Christmas Eves between midnight and two o'clock in the morning, Jack can be heard gibbering about the white deer and the halo of light. And at the break of dawn on Christmas morning, the young red buck and Jack's dog can be seen near where his body was found. Crockett's story has been verified by many area hunters who claim that they have fired their guns at the deer but have never hit him. The dog and the buck then vanish in the underbrush.

The Vanishing Cemetery

It was during the Depression, in the late 1930s, when a young couple moved from the Midwest to Tidewater Virginia. The husband had been lucky. He had gotten a job through the Works Progress Administration to survey drainage ditches surrounding the Great Dismal Swamp. He and his wife seemed to have a deep attraction for the mystic beauty of the swamp. They often walked is paths and trails on weekends.

One day, the young man was out walking alone while his wife stayed home tending to a sick child. He followed an abandoned and overgrown logging trail. Presently, he came upon a small family graveyard. He knelt down beside the ancient tombstones, dating from the late eighteenth century. He knew that his wife would enjoy seeing the old markers. So, as he backtracked, he carefully marked the spot where he had made his discovery. The entrance was next to some live oak trees, past a clump of three hollies and the stump of an old pine that had been splintered by lightning. He then counted his paces back along the logging road.

The following Sunday, he excitedly took his wife down the trail. He passed the stump and the holly trees and turned into where he had found the tombstones. There was nothing there! Instead, the couple found only an open, clear glade. The man was thoroughly puzzled. He rechecked his markings. He was sure that this was the exact spot. They searched for hours, to no avail, and finally had to return home when darkness began to fall.

The next day, the man went to Sam Smith's general store and told Smith about what had happened. Smith smiled and nodded. He said that he had heard the same story many times. He told the man that if you go looking for the graveyard, you never can find it. It may be there, because a few people have stumbled upon it, Smith said, but no one has ever found it twice.

AN OMNIBUS OF OLDE TOWNE HAUNTS

The Olde Towne section of Portsmouth, Virginia, is a fascinating, well-preserved repository of some of the most elegant early American architecture in the nation, with superb examples of Colonial, Federal, Greek Revival, Georgian and Victorian houses. Homeowners obviously have taken great pride in their dwellings, yards and gardens in this one-square-mile antique oasis, and there is enough wrought-iron flavor to remind one of New Orleans's famous French Quarter.

Olde Towne is also a psychic gold mine, with one of the greatest concentrations of ghosts in the commonwealth. At last count, there was something like twenty-seven separate specters haunting the houses within this area of a few square blocks. And what a marvelous setting they have, amid all of the gargoyles and turrets, the dank basements and musty attics. The rich, colorful tales of the supernatural here have been told and retold for generations and have resulted in a popular annual ghost walk each Halloween week. Here, then, is a sampling of these regional spirits.

The Grieved Slave

In 1987, Cathi Bunn and her family moved into the historic Grice-Neely House at 202 North Street. The first portion of this English basement home is believed to have been built sometime in the 1750s, and it still contains some original wooden-pegged rafters. Interestingly, there is a place on the rear façade of the building where a rather large window has been bricked over. Cathi says that in the 1850s, a medium held a séance in the house and told the owners that when the next person living there died, they should be lowered out of this window, and then the window should be taken out and paved over with brick. By doing this, the family would forever ward off evil spirits.

The Grice-Neely House in Olde Towne Portsmouth houses the ghost of a murdered slave.

Cathi became personally acquainted with the resident ghost here in a somewhat frightening manner. "I was all alone one night," she recalls, "and I decided to take a nice hot bath. I left the door slightly ajar and was soaking when I heard footsteps in the hallway. I thought my husband and kids had come back, but it wasn't them. It sounded like someone with no shoes on. It came right up to the bathroom door and then stopped. I was scared. Then the steps continued, which was quite strange, because there was a solid wall where it kept walking!"

Cathi adds that earlier tenants of the house also met the ghost, one of them face to face. "A college student was staying in one of the bedrooms," she says, "and one night he woke up to find an African American man standing at the foot of his bed. Then 'he' dissolved, like a mist." A female tenant once saw the same apparition standing on the circular staircase. She froze when she realized that she could see right through him. There have been numerous other sightings. One resident was so frightened by the sounds of someone running across the attic floor above his room that he wanted to keep a gun by his bed. Cathi told him, "What's up there you can't shoot, because I think it's already dead."

In her efforts to track down the origins of the spirit and why it is still in the house, Cathi learned of a legend that clearly fits the description of what has been seen and heard over the years. It is, she believes, the ghost of a former slave named Jemmy, who was stabbed to death in the early 1800s by his master, who was having an illicit affair with Jemmy's wife. He periodically reappears, searching for her.

The Headless "Graduate"

The Ball-Nivison House in Olde Towne Portsmouth was built about 1780. Bob Albertson's family has lived there for more than three quarters of a century, and for a long time during this period there was a resident ghost here with very predictable habits. "We treated him just like another member of the family," Albertson says. "People can live with ghosts. They're not malevolent. He goes his way and I go mine. We never tried to pass it off as a haunted house, but I have to admit, a number of things have happened here that aren't supposed to happen, and I can't explain them."

The manifestations that he and others in the family have been subjected to seem to follow a precise pattern. The specter always goes one way, from the library to the hall door. There, it lifts a heavy antique latch-lock adorned

The Ball-Nivison House in Olde Towne Portsmouth is the scene of considerable paranormal activity, including the sighting of a headless ghost.

with a lion and unicorn, opens the door, walks up the steps and stops by a bedroom door. "I can tell you this," Albertson says. "That latch is so heavy it couldn't blow open or open by itself."

Only Albertson's mother has seen the spirit, and she says that it was without a head. She saw it once more than forty years ago. It appeared to her wearing a black robe similar to a graduation gown, and it seemed to make the sound of labored breathing. She said that there was something like a mortar board resting atop its shoulders. "For many years, I have heard of a legend of a headless horseman riding down Glasgow Street in the dead of night," Albertson says. "Our house is almost at the foot of Glasgow. People can make what they want of it."

A Prophesy of Death

How would you like to know the precise day on which you would die? That, apparently, is what happened to Reverend John Braidfoot, a Scotsman who became the second rector of Trinity Church in Portsmouth in 1773. Following the Revolutionary War, during which he served as chaplain of the Continental army, Braidfoot had a difficult time maintaining his ministry. It

The grave site of Reverend Blaidfoot, in Portsmouth, who was told of the day he would die by a ghost.

was an era when many churches closed, but the reverend continued to live in the rectory at the Glebe and regularly visited his neighbors in need.

One night, while driving home in his buggy, his horse stopped suddenly. Blocking the road was what Braidfoot later described as an apparition. There was an eerie silence, and then, in a rare occurrence, the apparition spoke. It told the reverend that he would die at home on the following February 6. This grim prophesy was repeated three or four times over the next few months.

According to the reverend's great-granddaughter, who recounted the legend a century and a half later, Braidfoot's wife decided to have a dinner party on February 6 to take her husband's mind off of death. In the midst of the festivities, the reverend excused himself and went up to his room. When he did not return, members of the party went up to look for him.

He was dead!

The Girl Who Was "Born to See"

"She was," says Gabrielle Bielenstein, "'born to see.' Isn't that a marvelous expression? It means, of course, that a person is psychic. Some people are born with perfect pitch, and some can play the piano by ear. She was 'born to see.'"

Gabrielle is talking—in the darkened, high-ceilinged parlor of her magnificent Art Nouveau home at 328 Court Street in Olde Towne Portsmouth—about the teenage African American girl who worked for Gabrielle's mother more than half a century ago. It is called the Maupin House, the family name, and it was built in 1885 because Gabrielle's grandmother, Edmonia, wanted to live on Court Street, since it was the most fashionable section of the city. The house has about twenty rooms, including six bathrooms, a beautiful spiral staircase and exquisite wood paneling throughout. Behind it was a splendid walled garden.

Gabrielle and her identical twin sister grew up in the house, and the young girl came to work here in the early 1940s, during World War II. Almost immediately, she began to "see" things that others didn't. "There had been some strange occurrences in the house before," Gabrielle says, "but we never paid much attention to them. One would hear tales. Some of the other servants would talk occasionally about a rocking chair rocking on its own on the front porch. We would hear noises that sounded like someone descending the staircase when no one was there. Things like that."

The Maupin House in Olde Towne Portsmouth was the site where a servant girl displayed psychic abilities far beyond the normal five senses.

The new girl, however, saw, felt and sensed presences in and around the house almost from the day she began work. And, with uncanny accuracy, they perfectly fit descriptions of past residents, both animal and human. Consider, for example, the buried pit bulls. "My mother, Florence, had about given up on having any children before my sister and I came along, so she had lots of pets," Gabrielle says. "Now, you have to understand this was at a time when these dogs were very rare. Few people knew what they looked like."

She continued:

> *My mother didn't have much luck, and most of them died very young and they were all buried in little pine coffins in a corner of the yard. When the young girl came to work for us, there hadn't been any pit bulls around for years, and I don't believe she had any way of knowing what they looked like. Yet she told us she saw the dogs playing in the yard. When she was asked to describe what they looked like, she said they were just like Miss Julia's dog. Miss Julia was a neighbor who had a Boston Terrier, which closely resembles a pit bull. How did she know what those dogs looked like unless she saw them?*

The girl also saw the apparition of Miles Portlock. Born a slave before the Civil War, he had been a servant to Gabrielle's great-grandmother. "We considered him a part of the family, and as a child I can remember him sitting at the kitchen table and drinking ice tea," Gabrielle says. "He died about 1939 or 1940, somewhere around the age of ninety, well before the girl came to Maupin House to work. Yet she said that she saw him in the garden with his cane, and she described him perfectly, too."

And then there were the sightings of Miss Edmonia, Gabrielle's grandmother. The girl said that she saw an "old woman" on the staircase at times. Gabrielle explains:

> *We had a lot of photos in the house in those days, but there were no recent photos of Edmonia before her death, because she refused to have any taken after she reached middle age. She had been a beautiful woman.*
>
> *We took the girl around to view all the photos, and she immediately picked out an earlier portrait of Edmonia, and said that was who she saw. She said it was the same person, only she was much older now. How did she know? How did she pick that one picture out of all the ones in the house? She had no way of knowing what Edmonia looked like. I can't explain it.*

Gabrielle Bielenstein, mistress of the Maupin House in Olde Towne Portsmouth, tells of the young girl who once lived there and displayed rare psychic abilities.

The Maupin House is one of the most popular stops on the annual Olde Towne Ghost Walk at Halloween. Someone always plays the part of old Miles Portlock and tells the stories of the ghostly legends and the young girl who was "born to see."

THE MAD POLTERGEIST OF PORTSMOUTH

It was known simply as the house on Florida Avenue in the Mount Hermon section of Portsmouth, Virginia. It was torn down several years ago. It probably is just as well. There was a time, half a century ago, when the old house at 949 Florida Avenue was the talk not only of the town but also of the entire country. For a brief period in September 1962, the residence became a whirlwind of psychic activity that lasted several days, frightened the wits out of the chief of police and newspaper reporters, among others, and drew unruly crowds of thousands who demanded to see what was going on.

It had begun, innocently enough, on a Thursday afternoon about 4:00 p.m. Charles and Annie Daughtery were living in the house at the time with their great-great-grandson. The Daughterys were described as being very old; Annie was said to be close to one hundred. A little horse vase, sitting on a sewing machine in the hallway, fell on the floor three or four times. Annie, who said that she didn't know what ghosts or haunted houses were, and was not afraid of them, told her great-great-grandson to take the vase and set it outside. Just then, a bottle of hair lotion inexplicably sailed through the air and struck her in the back of the head.

By the next day, accounts of the mysterious happenings had circulated throughout the neighborhood and beyond and had come to the attention of local newspaper reporters. It had been alleged that a carpet eerily rose off the floor by itself; vases jumped from mantelpieces and hurtled over people's heads; and a mattress slid off a bed and onto a floor, all in front of the incredulous Annie. The phenomena had not been witnessed by her alone. Friends and neighbors had seen these occurrences, too, although many didn't stay long. They had fled in stark fear. One who reportedly had run out of the house was the local chief of police.

By Saturday, the events had become so celebrated that when Joseph Phillips, a Norfolk newspaper staff writer, entered the house along with a photographer, a mob of more than two hundred people had gathered outside. "I didn't believe in ghosts—until Saturday," Phillips began his front-page article. But, he added, he "got goose pimples while dodging flying household objects that crashed to bits on the floor. I saw weird things happen, but I don't know what caused them."

When Phillips entered the house, he stood by a buffet with Mrs. Marion Bivens, a neighbor. She asked him if he had felt the buffet move. She looked scared. He hadn't felt anything. Suddenly, a vase that had been on the mantelpiece in the living room crashed into the hallway wall at the front of the house, apparently rounding a corner in the process. Phillips and the photographer ran to the living room. There was no one there. As they ran, a cup from the buffet in the dining room shattered at their feet. At this point, Mrs. Bivens ran from the house in terror.

"Then I saw an empty tobacco can fly toward me from the buffet," Phillips said. "It was in the air when I saw it. It crashed and rolled to the floor at my feet." Phillips's subsequent story of his experience drew even more people to the area, and when a wire service article ran a day or two later, crowds grew to enormous proportions. Police estimated that twenty thousand curious onlookers congregated there one day, and they ordered out the fire department, hoses ready, in case a riot broke out. Some in the horde of people stormed inside the house and demanded to "see the thing." Several were arrested, and finally the Daughterys had to move out of the house and stay with relatives until the excitement died down.

William G. Roll, then a student with the Parapsychology Lab at Duke University, showed up to investigate. He said that there were enough witnesses to support the likelihood that the disturbances in the house were caused by recurrent spontaneous psychokinesis, or RSPK. Roll claimed that the flying objects and loud noises were not necessarily the work of a ghost. Rather, he believed that they were the work of the living, not the dead.

"Our focus on RSPK eruptions has been on the individual who is at the center of the disturbances," he told a reporter, adding that usually such occurrences are sparked by tension or certain neurological features. Maybe so, but that was a difficult theory to swallow by any of the scores of people who were in the little house on Florida Avenue during the few days when all hell broke loose. They didn't have a rational explanation, but they knew what they saw. As reporter Phillips summed it up, "I didn't believe this nonsense before. Now I'm not so sure."

A MOTHER'S LAST GOODBYE

The late Roger Rageot, a native Frenchman who lived in Norfolk, Virginia, most of his life, was first and foremost a naturalist, but he also could be called an explorer, author, photographer, artist and a museum officer. For example,

Roger Rageot. *Illustration by Brenda Goens.*

he was curator of the Norfolk Museum of Natural History from 1951 until its closing in 1967. He also had a fascination with the supernatural and once told of a touching psychic event he personally experienced when he was still with the museum.

Late one winter evening, Roger and a friend were talking in his office when the doorbell rang unexpectedly.

I got up to open the door. There stood my mother! A four-inch snowfall lay on the ground, and she stood so small and frail, with snowflakes blowing around her. There is nothing really unusual about one's mother ringing your doorbell late at night. But I knew my mother was dying of bone cancer, a continent away, in a hospital in Paris, France! And I was in Norfolk, Virginia.

I stood in stupefaction! I'll never know what made me say what I said to her. Maybe it was the strange look on her face, a very peculiar smile, one common to a contented person. Her eyes were vacant, possessing an indescribable light. They appeared almost phosphorescent. I could see that her mind was transported into another, more distant world. She didn't speak.

"When did you die?" I blurted out. She chuckled shyly and replied, "How do you know I'm dead? Didn't I tell you I'd come over to America someday? Well, here I am."

At this point, Roger's friend, Roland Young, interrupted and said, "I don't know what you two are trying to put over on me, but I simply refuse to believe any of it."

"But this is my mother, Roland," Roger said. "How could you not believe it?" Roland then replied, "Your mother's sick. How could she have traveled over here?"

"She's dead!" Roger declared.

Roger and his mother then started reminiscing and soon were so lost in remembering the past that Roland's presence in the room was completely forgotten. Sometime later, Roger's mother said, "It's getting late, son, and I still must see your sister in Kentucky. I'd better leave now."

Roger said, "She then arose and handed me something. I accompanied her to the front door and was about to bid her goodbye, but she suddenly vanished. I turned to Roland, who stood transfixed. He stared at the spot where, only a few seconds ago, my mother had stood. 'What did she give you?' he asked."

"Until then, I hadn't noticed," Roger continued. "I opened my closed fist. It was a tiny locket, one that I had given her when I was a little child. There was an inscription on it which read, 'To Mommy, with love, Roger.' I showed it to Roland, who said this was all too much for him. 'Well,' I replied, 'You and I have often discussed the realm of the supernatural. It is everywhere. It surrounds us, it even penetrates us. Science tries constantly to pursue it, but cannot even get near it.'"

"The day after my mother's apparition appeared, I received a letter from my father, in Paris," Roger said. "'My dear son,' he wrote, 'Because the news that I'm about to bring you will cause you much pain, you must have great courage. I'm sorry to relate that your devoted mother passed away yesterday.'"

Roger concluded his description of the incident by saying, "I have often participated in intellectual discussions of the paranormal. I used to participate theoretically. But my experience with my mother's apparition has changed things. Now I discuss the supernatural with confidence and some authority."

A Case of Crisis Apparition

It is a shaded, secluded isle of serenity amid the hustle and bustle of downtown Norfolk. It has been that way for more than 350 years. In fact, the first church built on the site of the present-day St. Paul's was known as "Ye Chappell of Ease." It was erected in 1641 as part of the Elizabeth River Parish. Norfolk became a borough in 1736, and the present church was built in 1739.

The building was assailed and partially burned by the British on January 1, 1776, when Norfolk was bombarded and destroyed. The church was serving as a shelter for women and children during the attack. In the Civil War, Federal forces occupied the church from 1862 to 1865. The 1.75-acre churchyard is similar to the old yards of England. There are 274 listed graves here, the oldest belonging to Dorothy Farrell, who died on January 18, 1673. Some of the stone markers bear a skull and crossbones, which simply signified death rather than the resting place of a pirate. Wedged into the far northeast corner of the churchyard is an above-ground tombstone with a strange quotation carved into it.

"Yes," says a church spokesman when asked, "that was a tragic case. The poor man lost his whole family. It is our only ghost story." It also was, apparently, a case of crisis apparition. This occurs when a person, the "receiver," suddenly becomes aware that another person, the "transmitter," is undergoing a crisis. This may be in the form of pain, shock, emotion or death, even though the transmitter may be some distance away, in some cases thousands of miles. The most common examples of such phenomena occur in times of war, when a mother, for instance, may report seeing or hearing her son at the moment he is wounded or at the instant of his death. The theory goes that the pain and shock trigger involuntary telepathic contact between mother and son, or transmitter and receiver.

David Duncan's crisis apparition occurred in 1823. Three years earlier, he had married Martha Shirley, the daughter of a widow who operated the Norfolk boardinghouse, where he often stayed. Duncan was captain of the

This unusual headstone, located in the cemetery of St. Paul's Church in downtown Norfolk, marks the burial site of the wife and children of sea captain David Duncan. It represents a dramatic case of crisis apparition that occurred in 1823.

cargo schooner *Sea Witch*, and he took his bride on a honeymoon voyage to several Mediterranean ports. Afterward, they settled in Norfolk, and she gave birth to twins, Davis and Ann. Early in 1823, Duncan set sail again on a merchant voyage, carrying a cargo of lumber and animal hides.

On the night of May 12, the *Sea Witch* was anchored in the harbor of Genoa, Italy. Most of the crew had gone ashore to unwind, but Duncan had stayed behind and was in his cabin reading a book, *Night Thoughts on Life, Death, and Immortality*, by the English poet Edward Young. It was eerily apropos.

Thousands of miles away, a fire broke out in the bakery beneath the rooms occupied by Mrs. Duncan and her children. Martha desperately tried to escape with her infants, but a rickety staircase collapsed, and they perished in the flames. At that precise instant, David Duncan was reading the poet's lines that described death as an "insatiate archer" when he envisioned a fire at the foot of the main mast. He ran from his cabin, and when he reached the deck, the fire seemed to blossom. In the midst of the flames, he clearly saw the wraithlike form of his wife frantically clutching their son and daughter.

Her screams pierced the silence in the harbor. "David! David! Save us!" she cried. And then, in a flash, she was gone, as was the fire. Although crazed with anxiety, it was not until weeks later, when his ship finally docked at Norfolk, that Duncan learned that the awful horror of his vision was real.

And so he placed a horizontal raised tombstone, inscribed with Martha's name and the date of death, over a single grave site in St. Paul's churchyard. To this, he had the stonemason carve the two lines of verse he had been reading when his loved ones died: "Insatiate archer, could not one suffice? Thy shaft flew thrice and thrice my peace was slain."

PART VII

VIRGINIA BEACH AREA

THE LEGEND OF THE NORWEGIAN LADY

Tens of thousands of tourists in Virginia Beach pass by the bronze statue of *The Norwegian Lady* at Twenty-fifth Street and Oceanfront each summer without knowing the gripping and incredibly sad story of why the figure is there.

The saga began on the morning of March 3, 1891, when Captain J.M. Jorgensen sailed out of Pensacola, Florida, on the small Norwegian three-masted bark *Dictator*, bound for England with a cargo of yellow pine lumber. The ship carried a crew of fifteen, along with Jorgensen's wife, Johanne Pauline, and their four-year-old son, Karl.

Three weeks later, just north of the Bahama Islands, the *Dictator* ran headlong into a violent nor'easter storm and was unmercifully buffeted both by nearly hurricane-force winds and mountainous seas. Two of five lifeboats were swept overboard and lost in the surging ocean, and the ship sprung a leak. The captain wanted to attempt to ride out the storm, but the crew, described as disgruntled, virtually forced Jorgensen to alter his course and head toward Hampton Roads, Virginia, to make repairs.

On the morning of March 27, the ship, suffering greatly from the pounding waves, was sighted off Virginia Beach. By 9:30 a.m., crowds had gathered as it passed by the Princess Anne Hotel on Sixteenth Street.

According to eyewitness accounts, the spectators watched in horror as the *Dictator* struggled helplessly north. A little over an hour later, it foundered on a sandbar about three hundred yards offshore.

The situation was now desperate. A lifesaving crew first attempted to cannon-shoot a breeches buoy line to the ship, but this failed due to the excessively high winds. By now, two of the three remaining lifeboats had also been lost. Captain Jorgensen then decided to send four of his men in the remaining boat, and somehow they miraculously made it through the crashing surf to safety. Finally, after many unsuccessful attempts, a line from the beach to the ship was secured to the top of the main mast, and a breeches buoy was sent out in hopes of rescuing those remaining aboard.

But the ship was rolling so much in the high seas that the line would tighten and then slacken with each wave, either dunking a crew member into the ocean or throwing him high in the air. Despite this, however, the first

man made it to the beach unharmed. Jorgensen then told his wife and son to try it; paralyzed with fear, she refused. So another sailor was dispatched and reached shore. Two more made it safely before darkness halted the buoy operation.

The *Dictator*, having been pounded by the angry surf all day, began breaking up. As a last resort, the captain had his son strapped to his back, and they lowered themselves into the water, littered with loose boards of pine lumber. The surging sea quickly tore little Karl from his father's back, and he drowned. So, too, did a sailor and Mrs. Jorgensen. The captain was washed ashore and found unconscious but alive.

The statue of *The Norwegian Lady*, on the boardwalk in Virginia Beach, was erected to note a dramatic sea tragedy more than a century ago—one with haunting overtones.

The next day, the figurehead of the *Dictator*, a carved wooden robust woman, was found and placed on the boardwalk as a memorial to those who had lost their lives. The bodies of the crewmen who didn't make it, as well as Mrs. Jorgensen's, were then buried at Elmwood Cemetery in Norfolk. Little Karl's body was not found for several days, until a beachcomber saw it washed up near Seventeenth Street. The local man who discovered it didn't realize that this was Jorgensen's son, so he took Karl to his minister at a church south of Rudee Inlet, and the remains were buried there.

Within days, the eerie sounds of a child crying for his mother were heard at the cemetery by a number of witnesses. After this phenomenon repeated itself for several days, it was learned that the captain's son's body had not been found with the others, and the connection was made. Karl's body was exhumed and reburied next to his mother at Elmwood Cemetery. When this happened, the ghostly cries of the child were no longer heard in Virginia Beach.

The figurehead of the Norwegian lady decayed over the years and was replaced in 1962 by a bronze memorial created by Norway's famed sculptor, Oernulf Bast. And so she stands today, gazing out at the ocean, the scene so many years ago of a stark tragedy that took some lives but, by the heroic efforts of Virginia Beach citizens, saved several others.

An Obsession Named Melanie

Mary Bowman is a vivacious, red-haired, admitted workaholic who for years ran a successful interior design business in Virginia Beach. She also is "metaphysical." "If you are open," she explains, "you go beyond the five senses, which are earthbound." The layperson would call Mary a psychic, and she wouldn't argue. She has had such a special sensitivity since childhood. When she was ten, for example, she had a vivid dream in which her grandfather died. She awoke and told her parents. They told her to go back to sleep. An hour later, the telephone rang, and the family was informed of her grandfather's death.

Nothing in the conscious or paranormal world, however, prepared her for what happened in the fall of 1985. After working late at her office one night, she got in her car and headed home. As she was driving by the old John B. Dey farm on Greatneck Road, she suddenly felt a strange sensation.

"There was a voice," she remembers. "It was a young woman's voice, and it was crying out for help." It sounded urgent, and it seemed like the voice had singled out Mary for a specific purpose.

As time went on, the sensation grew stronger. Each time she drove past that section of the city, she would hear the girl calling out. Mary began to form a mental image. "It scared me at first," she says. "I saw a picture of a young girl, maybe eighteen or nineteen. She had long blonde hair and was lying down, as if she were in a coffin. She appeared to be wearing colonial-era clothes. She had billowing sleeves, and I got the strong feeling that she lived two hundred years ago."

There were other distinct features in Mary's mental picture. She envisioned a big, meandering farmhouse, with a large porch in white latticework, part of which was broken, and a very clear image of a brick wall. Somehow, Mary felt, all of these things were connected. "I became obsessed," she says. "I took off from work in the middle of the day and drove around looking for the house and brick wall. Things got crazy. I had to find out about the girl. Who was she? What did she want? Why was she calling me? I became a nervous wreck."

Mary consulted a well-known psychic counselor in Virginia Beach, but that proved inconclusive. She was then referred to Kay Buchanan, who also was psychically gifted. "She saw the same thing I did," Mary notes. "We felt the name of the girl was Melanie and that she might have been a schoolteacher. We somehow sensed she had an affair with a married man, and he had killed her and hastily buried her in an unmarked grave."

It was at this point that Mary says she had to let go. "I wanted to help, but it had become so overpowering I was afraid the search for Melanie would consume me." For the next several months, Mary tried to block out the vision and the sounds.

Then, one day, as she was out in the area of the old Dey farm, she saw it: the wall! The brick wall just as she had visualized it! It surrounded a farmhouse. Mary instinctively went up to the door and knocked. When the owner answered, she blurted out the story of her obsessive dream, including the vision of the brick wall.

"I was afraid the man would think I had escaped from the mental ward, but he didn't even seem surprised," Mary says. "In fact, he just said, 'I've got something to show you.' He led me into the garage, and there on the floor was a pile of human bones. He said some housing developers nearby had unearthed some unmarked graves in their diggings, and he had rescued the remains and was going to have them properly reburied. Everything became clear to me all of a sudden. That was why Melanie had been calling to me for help. She had been trying to tell me that." She added that the girl must have found peace at last with the reburial, because from that instant on Mary never again experienced the vision and the voice.

THE NON-GHOSTS OF THOROUGHGOOD HOUSE

Is Thoroughgood House in Virginia Beach haunted?

"Definitely not!" says Alice Tripp, a historical interpreter who worked at the house for several years.

"Yes, it was haunted even before it was opened to the public," declares Martha Bradley, the first curator at the house.

"No; oh, you might hear a creak or a strange noise from time to time—after all it is a very old house and you should expect that. But I never experienced anything out of the ordinary in all my years there," adds Nancy Baker, another historical interpreter.

"Yes, it is haunted. I can tell you for a fact there is at least one ghost or more there, because I personally experienced presences once, and it scared the life out of me," states Cindy Tatum, who once worked a summer at the house while she attended college.

And so, the argument continues. Present-day hostesses contend that there is nothing to the legends, while others who worked or visited here swear that there is, or was, spectral phenomena associated with the house. What no one disagrees with is that Adam Thoroughgood and his house are both fascinating in their own rights. Captain Adam arrived in the Virginia colony in 1621 as an indentured servant. He worked hard and did well. By 1626, he had purchased 150 acres of land on the Southampton River.

For his recruitment of 105 new settlers in 1635, he was awarded 5,350 acres of land along the western shore of the Lynnhaven River. That Thoroughgood was a prominent citizen is also established. He was named one of the original eight commissioners to Elizabeth City County, the shire from which New Norfolk and eventually Princess Anne was formed. He also was a burgess and a member of the governor's council.

There are, however, differing accounts as to actually when the house, said to be the oldest brick house in America, was constructed. Some historians have estimated that Adam built it as early as 1636, three years

The historic Adam Thoroughgood House in Virginia Beach is one of the oldest homes in America and is the site of poltergeist activity that has frightened workers and tourists alike.

before he died. But according to the fact sheet visitors are given today, the house probably was built by one of his descendants about 1660. It is a one-and-a-half-story structure made of brick and oyster shell mortar, with huge chimneys at each end.

It was sometime after a major renovation in 1957 when the ghostly manifestations began to surface. Charles Thomas Cayce—grandson of the great psychic Edgar Cayce and now head of the Association for Research and Enlightenment in Virginia Beach—says that the ARE has received calls at times about "strange experiences" at the house, particularly in an upstairs bedroom. The callers were curious, Cayce noted, but they didn't want to publicize it. He adds that his father, Hugh Lynn Cayce, and a physician friend of his once went to the house to look into some of the reported encounters. "A lady told them of seeing things fly off shelves, of little glass objects falling to the floor and of furniture being moved around when no one was in the house," Charles Thomas Cayce says.

Mrs. Bradley says that old-timers in the area told her of seeing a woman standing in the window with a lit candle before the house was opened to the public. After it was opened, she and other tour guides experienced all sorts of unexplained activities. As she showed the house to a party, including the wife of the ambassador of Denmark, Mrs. Bradley is quoted as saying, "All of us saw a candlestick actually move." She adds that children reported the sighting of a "small man in a brown suit" A lawyer visiting from Texas also claimed to have seen on oddly dressed little man.

And there have been other apparent poltergeist-type movements. Windows mysteriously open and close when no one is standing nearby. Tapes recorded in the house turn out blank. Once, in front of thirty tourists, four glass domes protecting Christmas candles suddenly levitated and crashed to the floor.

The person possibly most affected by all of this is Mrs. Tatum. She worked at the house giving tours in 1972, when she was seventeen. She says that there are a lot of stories about the place that are not told during tours. One is that it may well have been the first house of ill repute in the United States. "After all," she says, "it is on Pleasure House Road." She also tells of the resident who shot himself in the head halfway up the stairwell sometime in the 1700s. "We never talked about that to visitors, but it may be his ghost which comes back," Cindy adds. "Actually, there was more than one violent death in the house. A psychic came through one day and said she sensed an unhappy, trapped spirit."

Cindy says that when she worked there, the curator told her they had a few spiritual readings and table tappings in the evenings and that at times the table would rock violently. On another occasion during that eventful summer, she recalls coming in one morning when the hostesses found all of the upstairs furniture pushed up against the walls, as if someone had cleared the room for a dance. "There were some heavy pieces of furniture, too. We couldn't even move them." Cindy also tells of the inexplicable cold drafts on one side of the kitchen during the July heat with no air conditioning in the house and of rush lamps that would "singe up" without being lit.

But the occurrence that convinced her beyond a doubt that there was a ghostly presence in the house took place just before closing late one afternoon as she took a group of about fifteen visitors to the master bedroom upstairs:

> *I was standing inside the doorway with my back to the room, talking to the group. All of a sudden, several of the women started screaming, and then they began running down the stairs. I turned around, and you could see the bed being depressed as if someone was sitting or lying down on it! This is the truth. There was a definite indentation at least a foot deep.*
>
> *I began screaming, too. We all ran outside, and we closed the house for the day. A couple of the women later said they saw the vision of a small man on the bed. I didn't see that, but I did see the impression being made.*

I became hysterical. It really upset me. I'll never forget it as long as I live. My father, who is a minister, didn't want me to go back to the house. He said you don't mess with demons!

Edgar Cayce's Ghosts

He is universally recognized as the greatest American psychic of the twentieth century. He was also known as the "Sleeping Prophet," the "Psychic Diagnostician" and the "Miracle Worker of Virginia Beach." For more than forty years, Edgar Cayce helped save lives, cure incurable ailments and otherwise heal the sick through detailed "readings" he gave while in a trancelike state. Two-thirds of his more than fourteen thousand readings were medically related.

Though he had no more than an eighth-grade education, Cayce, while asleep, somehow had the ability to envision and diagnose the sicknesses, no matter how complicated, of people all over the country. Then, in precise, meticulous and sophisticated detail, he would prescribe the medicines and/ or treatments essential to each patient's return to full health. Often, such prescriptions included lengthy and complex medical terminology and, at times, obscure or long-forgotten remedies of which Cayce had no knowledge when awake. Astoundingly, of those cases verified by patients' reports, 85 percent of the diagnoses were found to be completely accurate, and those who followed the prescribed treatments got the satisfactory results predicted in the readings.

Consider, for example, a few sample case studies. In one instance, he gave a reading for a man who had been confined to an insane asylum for three years following a nervous breakdown, caused, it had been suspected, by nervous tension. In the reading, Cayce said, "Through pressures upon nerve energies in the coccyx area and the ileum plexus, as well as that pressure upon the lumbar axis, there had been a deflection of coordination between the sympathetic and the cerebrospinal nervous system."

He further diagnosed that the man's condition had actually been damaged by a spinal injury incurred by a fall. He didn't need psychotherapy. Instead, Cayce advised osteopathic adjustment and mild, specially outlined electrotherapy to normalize the disrupted nerve forces. The treatment was followed, and the results were dramatically successful. The man regained excellent health within six months and returned to a normal life.

Cayce's wife, Gertrude, once suffered from what doctors had determined as incurable tuberculosis. He gave her a reading and prescribed a diet, some simple drugs and a bizarre, unheard-of treatment: she was to inhale brandy fumes from a charred oak keg. Remarkably, it worked, and Mrs. Cayce recovered from her "incurable" disease.

One of the most amazing cures effected by the readings involved a young girl who had suddenly gone mad. Her condition did not respond to any of the treatments administered at the hospital. In desperation, her parents turned to Cayce for help. In his sleep state, he described the trouble as an impacted wisdom tooth that was disrupting nerve and brain function. He said that when the tooth was removed, the trouble would disappear. He had never seen the girl. He was four hundred miles away from the hospital where she was staying, yet when a dentist examined her, the impaction was found exactly as outlined. The dentist removed the tooth. Four hours later, the girl had regained her normal state of mind and never again showed any symptoms of mental disturbance.

To further his work for the benefit of mankind—Cayce never profited in a material sense from his psychic powers—he founded in 1931 the Association for Research and Enlightenment at Sixty-seventh Street and Atlantic Avenue in Virginia Beach. Today, the ARE, headed by his grandson, Charles Thomas Cayce, has more than 100,000 members worldwide and is dedicated to physical, mental and spiritual self-improvement programs through researching and applying the information in Cayce's psychic readings.

Edgar Cayce is widely recognized as the greatest American psychic in history. He also had numerous contacts with ghosts during his lifetime. *Courtesy of the Association for Research and Enlightenment.*

Eventually, in addition to medical diagnoses, the scope of his readings expanded to include data and advice on about ten thousand different subjects. These included such topics as world religions, philosophy, psychology, dreams, history, reincarnation, soul growth, diet and nutrition, spiritual development and the fabled lost continent of Atlantis, among others. When he died in 1945, Edgar Cayce left a legacy of readings that have stood the test of decades of intensive research, investigation and study. He remains the most documented psychic of all time.

Paranormal Experiences

Did Cayce ever have any encounters with spirits? Yes, says Charles Thomas Cayce. "I was only three when my grandfather died, so I can only tell you what I heard from members of the family and friends. My father, Hugh Lynn Cayce, and my uncle, Edgar Evans Cayce, mentioned stories about my grandfather communicating with ghosts. Are there such things as ghosts? The answer is yes. Some people are talented or gifted in ways of communicating with spirits. They are psychically talented in the same way a person may be musically or athletically gifted."

Vada F. Carlson, in a short composition on the early life of Edgar Cayce titled "The Vision of the Promise," said that Cayce saw and played with a whole group of ghostly playmates, both boys and girls:

> *It was disappointing to him that the grownups could not see the "play people" with whom he had so much fun, but Anna Seay, a small girl who lived nearby and came over to play with him, saw them as well as he did. She and Edgar played happily with them in woodsy places and in the cool shade of the barn. Edgar's mother believed him when he told her about the invisible children. His mother was the one person in the world who completely understood him. One day she glanced out the window and saw them waiting in the yard for him. "Go play with your friends," she told him. "They're waiting." It made Edgar very happy to know that she, too, could see the children.*

Cayce, Carlson reported, seemed amazed that his spectral friends could run in the rain without getting wet, and he wondered why they always disappeared whenever adults came near. Once Edgar was talking and laughing in the field when his father came by and asked him who he was talking to. "My friends," he told him. "Where are they?" asked his father. "Right here," the boy said, pointing. But his father saw no one.

There are two specific references in Edgar Cayce's authorized biography, written by his longtime friend Thomas Sugrue, relating to ghosts. One involved the death of his grandfather when Edgar was a small boy of five or six. They had been out horseback riding together, Grandpa in front and little Edgar behind him, holding on. They stopped at a pond to water the horse, and the boy slid off. Suddenly, the horse threw up its head, reared and plunged into deeper water. "We don't really know what happened," says Charles Thomas Cayce. "Perhaps it was frightened by a snake." The horse swam to the other side of the pond and raced to a fence, failed to jump it and galloped back to the pond, with Grandpa hanging on.

This time, the horse stumbled as it entered the water, and Grandpa was thrown over its head, landing on his back. The horse got to its feet, reared again and brought the full force of its fore hooves down on the old man's chest. Then it ran off. Grandpa's head was underwater. Young Edgar called to him, and when there was no answer, he ran for help, frightened. By then, however, it was too late. His grandfather was dead. Edgar said that even at that moment he could still talk with his grandfather, but in the excitement and grief, no one listened to him.

Later, Sugrue wrote, Edgar would see his grandfather "sometimes in the barns, usually when the tobacco was being fired. Of course, grandpa wasn't really there. You could see through him if you looked real hard." Edgar could only tell his mother and grandmother about the apparitional sightings, because he knew that it would have angered his father.

A Divine Spectacle

The second reference in the Sugrue biography to Cayce's spectral meetings occurred when Edgar was twelve years old. "When he was young, my grandfather spent a lot of time alone in the fields," says Charles Thomas. He would go out often to read his Bible. One afternoon in May, as he sat alone in the woods, reading the story of Manoah, he became aware of the presence of someone else.

Edgar looked up and saw a woman standing before him. At first, peering into the sun after reading, he thought it was his mother. But then the figure spoke, and he realized it was someone he did not know. "Her voice," wrote Sugrue, "was soft and very clear. It reminded him of music." The woman told him that his prayers had been answered, and she asked him what he would like most of all, so that she might give it to him. At first, he could not speak. He was frightened, especially when he noticed that she had shadows on her back shaped like wings. She reassured him by smiling. Finally, he managed to say that "most of all, I would like to be helpful to others, and especially to children when they are sick." Then, suddenly, the woman was gone.

Edgar ran home and told his mother of the ethereal experience. He said that maybe he had been reading the Bible too much and was losing his sanity. She told him that because he was such a good boy, "why shouldn't your prayers be answered?" They talked about the meaning of the apparitional visit. It might mean, she told her son, that he was destined to become a doctor or a preacher or possibly a missionary. Only later, when he became fully aware of his psychic powers, did he realize the true intent of his experience. It meant that he was to use those powers in a positive way to help others.

And the first true clue to his great gift came the next evening. He had done miserably at school that day, particularly in his spelling lessons. When he couldn't correctly spell the word "cabin," his teacher made him stay after school and write the word five hundred times on the blackboard. His father heard about the incident, and that night he told Edgar that he was a disgrace to the family. After supper, the boy and his father sat for hours, poring over the lesson book, and Edgar's answers were all wrong. Twice, Squire Cayce became so exasperated that he knocked the boy out of his chair.

Then, tired and sleepy, Edgar heard the voice of the woman he had seen the day before. She told him that if he could sleep a little, "we can help you." He begged his father to let him rest. He reluctantly agreed, telling Edgar that it would be his last chance. The squire then went into the kitchen for a few minutes, and Edgar almost instantly nodded off. When his father came back, Edgar woke up and told him that he knew his lessons. And he did. He got every word right. Not only that, he knew the assignment for the next day. In fact, by sleeping on his book, he had somehow, inexplicably, memorized every word and picture on every page in the book. He could envision the word, where it was on the page and what the illustrations were. When he spelled "synthesis" perfectly, the squire lost his temper and struck him again.

When Edgar told his mother about the episode the next day, and still knew every word on every page in the book, she said to him that she was sure the lady he had envisioned was keeping her promise. After that, Edgar would take other schoolbooks to bed, put them under his pillow and sleep on them, and the next day he would know everything in the book. When his befuddled father asked him how he did it, he told him that he didn't know, but it worked. Was the angel an apparition or a dream? "I'm not sure," says Charles Thomas. "But I was told it was something he experienced while he was awake, so I don't think it was a dream."

Talking with the Dead

Cayce apparently had a number of encounters with ghosts during his adult years as well, and although this is not specifically addressed in his readings, Charles Thomas says that his father, Hugh Lynn Cayce, remembered Edgar talking about such incidents at times. In a lecture series, in fact, Hugh Lynn told of the gentle tapping one evening at a downstairs window. Edgar rose from his bed to go down and see who it was. It was an apparition, because Hugh Lynn wrote: "It seemed to Edgar a perfectly natural procedure to get up, go downstairs, unlock the front door and let in a rather diffident young woman—who had been quite dead a few years!"

The woman told Cayce that she had died of a toxic throat infection without fully realizing she was dead and that she was having a terrible time adjusting to "the other side." In this confused state, she had haunted Cayce's former photographic studio in Selma, Alabama. When she found out that he had moved to Virginia Beach, she had traveled there to see if he could help her. He did. Hugh Lynn said that his father taught her how to release herself from what some people call "the earthbound condition" and to move forward in her path of development. "Edgar Cayce both saw and heard this girl," Hugh Lynn said. "Actually, he saw through her, because she wasn't exactly solid, but she was solid enough to ask for his help and to tap on the window loud enough to attract his attention."

Hugh Lynn himself, along with other members of his family, experienced a ghostly visitation in their house in Virginia Beach shortly after Squire Cayce, Hugh Lynn's grandfather, died. They heard "puttering around" upstairs when no one was up there. Edgar told everyone not to worry, that it was just his father "returning" to straighten out some papers before he "left." Edgar said to just leave him alone and he would be gone pretty soon. But Hugh Lynn couldn't resist the temptation. "I heard the noise so clearly," he said later. "I insisted on running upstairs to check." As he reached the landing, before getting to the top of the stairs, he felt a presence that he described as "a cold area, with a feeling like cobwebs." Hugh Lynn said that "every hair on my head stood at attention."

One evening in the fall of 1933, Edgar was alone downstairs in his Virginia Beach house, listening to the radio, when suddenly the room got icy cold, and he felt something "uncanny or unusual" taking place. When he looked toward the radio, he realized that a friend of his, who had been dead for several months, was sitting in front of the radio. Edgar said, "He turned and smiled at me, saying, 'There is the survival of personality. I know! And a life of service and prayer is the only one to live.'" Cayce added,

I was shaking all over. He said nothing more and just seemed to disappear. I turned off the radio. It still appeared as if the room was full of some presence. As I switched off the light and climbed the stairs, I could hear many voices coming from the darkened room. Jumping into bed and shivering from the cold, I aroused my wife. She asked me why I hadn't turned off the radio. I assured her I had. She opened the door and said, "I hear it. I hear voices." We both did.

Cayce wrote of the experience in a short monograph. He noted in it that this particular friend had been a corporate executive, and when the two of them had gotten together they often discussed whether or not there was a survival of personality after death. Cayce said that the friend would usually close the talk by saying, "Well, whichever one goes first will communicate with the other."

The most frightening paranormal manifestation Edgar Cayce ever experienced occurred in June 1936 on a bright sunny day, when he was hoeing in his garden. He heard a noise he described as sounding like a swarming of bees. Startled, he looked up and saw in the sky a chariot drawn by four white horses. Then he heard a voice saying, "Look behind you." When he did, he saw a man with a shield, helmet, knee guards and a cape, clad in burnished silver. The phantom figure raised his hand in salute and said, "The chariot of the Lord and the horsemen thereof." With that, the vision vanished. Cayce was so upset that he bolted into the house and locked himself in his study. Hours later, when he emerged, he said that what he witnessed signaled the approach of World War II and the death of millions.

There were a number of other ghostly incidents that involved Edgar Cayce during his lifetime. He seemed to attract spirits. His grandson, Charles Thomas Cayce, believes that one reason for this, in addition to Edgar's incredible psychic abilities, is the fact that he was located in Virginia Beach. "This site is near two large bodies of water," he says, "the Chesapeake Bay and the Atlantic Ocean. There is an implication about the energies of the area being particularly conducive to paranormal forces."

PART VIII

TIDEWATER MISCELLANY

TIDEWATER TICKLERS

In the gathering of paranormal encounters in Virginia over the past thirty years, I have occasionally come across some truly humorous incidents that involved people who perceived that they were witnessing real ghostly events when they were not. Fright often triggers such occurrences, and when the real or rational sources of supposed manifestations are revealed, it often leads to lighthearted laughter. Here are some true examples.

Hooded Visions Rise from the Mist

In the 1970s, in the midst of a severe winter, tourism was way down in historic Colonial Williamsburg, so one afternoon, when five historical interpreters were invited to visit an old church in neighboring New Kent County and learn of its history, they readily accepted. They were driven to the site, and because of the cold weather, they were wearing long hooded cloaks over their colonial costumes.

After the tour, they went outside and sat down on a bench in front of the little cemetery adjacent to the church to wait for their ride back to town. It was now nearing dark, and it was drizzling slightly. Pretty soon, they heard a vehicle coming up the country road. Assuming it was their ride, these five women in their costumes, with long cloaks and hoods, in the dusk and mist, arose in unison, with the shadowy tombstones in the background.

And it wasn't their ride. It was a tourist from New Jersey. The ladies said that he took one look at them and promptly drove into a tree.

The Civil War Soldier in the Cemetery

The following is told by Vincent Curtis of Chesapeake, Virginia, who has been a member of the North-South Skirmish Association since 1954. The NSSA is an organization of reenactors who dress in authentic reproduction Civil War uniforms and carry rifles, swords, knapsacks, haversacks and other accoutrements. Curtis says that he became fast friends with two longtime members, Jack Rawls and George Oswald.

One weekend about fifty-five years ago, the First Virginia Volunteers were to attend a shooting match in Petersburg, and Jack and George decided to drive there together. They felt it would be easier and quicker to just dress in their Confederate uniforms and other equipment at home instead of changing at the shoot and again afterwards. After the shoot, they got in their car and drove home to Norfolk.

Now there is a large cemetery in Norfolk facing Granby Street, and Jack lived behind it, facing another street. When they got to town, Jack told George to let him out at the main entrance to the cemetery, and he would walk home through it. That way, George could turn around and drive home instead of going all around the graveyard, which was a distance out of his way.

Jack got out, put on his hat, knapsack and haversack, hoisted his rifle over his shoulder and started to walk through the cemetery. George then drove down to a place where he could turn around and headed home. As he passed by the cemetery again, he saw a car had crashed through the fence on the other side, knocked over a tombstone and was lying on its side. Since he was in a hurry, and there already were some people gathered at the site, George didn't stop.

A few weeks later at a luncheon, George met the manager of the cemetery and asked him about the wreck he had seen. The manager said the driver of the vehicle was a sailor, and they suspected he had been drinking, because he kept trying to tell everyone he had lost control of his car when he saw a Confederate soldier walking among the tombstones!

The Corpse that Sat Up

Sometimes the dead are really dead, but the appearance is otherwise. Such a case is related by Mary Daughdrill of Norfolk. According to Mary, her grandfather ran a sizeable farming operation in the early 1900s despite suffering from a very severe physical handicap. He was a hunchback, and his impediment was so great that he was nearly doubled over when he walked. He died in 1915, and morticians had a difficult time fitting him into a casket. Mary says that they had to strap him in to get the lid to shut. They placed his casket on the back of a wagon and headed to church for services. The road, however, was deeply rutted, and it was a jarring ride.

The church was packed, not only with friends, relatives and loved ones but also with a large number of servants and fieldworkers who filled the back rows. At a point in the service, a gentleman went over to raise the lid of the coffin so that everyone could get a final view of the dearly departed.

Unbeknownst to the brethren, however, the jolting ride to the church apparently had loosened or broken the straps holding the body down. So when the lid was raised, the body popped bolt upright, causing instantaneous panic in the church. The building emptied in seconds.

She Didn't Really Want Him Back

On the Eastern Shore of Virginia, there is a popular legend about a woman who got her wish and then didn't want it. When her husband died in the early 1930s, she had him buried in the family cemetery, but it was hard for her to let him go. It was said you could hear her crying late at night, saying, "Oh Lord, send him back to me."

Several weeks later, a hurricane swept through the Chesapeake Bay, flooding the area at high tide. The storm unearthed the coffin of the woman's husband and washed it up to her doorstep!

When she saw it out the window, she allegedly screamed, "Oh Lord, I don't want him. I didn't mean it. Take him back!"

The Walking Skull

The following story was published in a letter to the editor published in the July 27, 1739 issue of the *Virginia Gazette*. The writer told of an incident that occurred when two men were digging a grave in a country church cemetery. One of their shovels hit something solid. It was a human skull. They brushed the dirt off it and laid it beside the grave.

To their utter shock and disbelief, both men saw the skull moving on its own. They raced to the little church and stammered what they had seen to the parson. He suspected that the men had been drinking while digging but came out to see for himself. Sure enough, the skull moved. The wide-eyed parson shouted, "It's a miracle!"

He immediately sent for a cross and some holy water and ordered the church bell to be rung. Curious parishioners flocked to the church. The skull was taken inside the building and laid on the altar, and there the intrigue was quickly solved.

A tiny mole crawled out of one of the skull's eye sockets. The gathered congregation members abruptly dispersed in all directions.

THE MYSTERY OF THE PINK ROSE PETALS

A few years ago, I was signing books at the annual Newport News Fall Festival. I was approached by a well-dressed middle-aged woman who said that she wanted to tell me something but that she knew I wouldn't believe it. I told her that I heard that a lot during my thirty years of collecting true ghostly experiences and to go ahead. This is what she related:

When I was a young girl of twelve, my grandmother died, and they buried her in a pearl-gray suit. As they were lowering her casket into the ground, I dropped three pink rose petals into the grave, because my grandmother had always loved pink roses.

Forty years later, I was in the hospital for a very serious cancer operation. They didn't know if I was going to live or die. I was in the intensive care ward, where no flowers and no visitors were allowed. As they were getting ready to take me into the operating room, a vision of my dead grandmother suddenly appeared, still in her pearl-gray suit. The vision spoke, saying, "Don't worry, you will live to see your children's children!" Then the figure vanished.

Just then the attendants entered the room. As they lifted me from the bed to a gurney to wheel me in for the operation, a nurse and I both saw three pink rose petals flutter to the floor.

BIBLIOGRAPHY

Barden, Thomas, ed. *Virginia Folk Legends*. Charlottesville: University Press of Virginia, 1991.

Bielenstein, Gabrielle. Personal interview, August 13, 1989.

Bowman, Mary. Personal interview, November 29, 1989.

Bunn, Cathi. Personal interview, August 12, 1989.

Carrington, Hereward. *Phantasm of the Dead*. New York: Dodd-Mead, 1920.

Carter, Hill. Personal interview, October 6, 1982.

Cayce, Charles Thomas. Personal interview, June 22, 1989.

Chewning, Alpheus. Personal interview, January 21, 2006.

Curtis, Vincent. Personal interview, September 24, 2000.

Daughdrill, Mary. Personal interview, March 8, 1993.

Davis, Herbert. "A Tragic Toast at Brandon." *Olde Towne Magazine*, October 1966.

Davis, Olivia. Personal interview, July 13, 1989.

Fisher, Moocie. Personal interview, November 12, 1982.

Gulbranson, Tom. Personal interview, May 9, 1989.

Hawkins, Samuel. Personal journal, Yorktown, Virginia, 1791.

Lanciano, Claude. *Rosewell, Garland of Virginia*. Gloucester, VA: Gloucester County Historical Society, 1978.

Lee, Marguerite. *Virginia Ghosts*. Richmond, VA: Byrd Press, 1930.

McDowell, Gerry. Personal interview, April 12, 1989.

Nock, Sam. Personal interview, September 4, 1989.

"Ordeal of Touch." Northampton County, Virginia court records, December 14, 1656.

Polonsky, Jane. *The Ghosts of Fort Monroe*. Hampton, VA: Polydrum Publications, 1972.

Rageot, Roger. "A Locket from the Dead." *Fate* magazine, November 1963.

Rollins, Randolph. Personal interview, August 1, 1989.

Tatum, Cindy. Personal interview, July 9, 1989.

Taylor, L.B., Jr. *Ghosts of Virginia*. Vols. 1 through 7. Lynchburg, VA: self-published, 1993–2000.

———. *Ghosts of Williamsburg*. Vols. 1 and 2. Lynchburg, VA: self-published, 1983–95.

Tucker, George. *Virginia Supernatural Tales*. Norfolk, VA: Donning Publishers, 1977.

Virginia Gazette. "The Walking Skull." July 27, 1739.

Waggoner, John. Personal interview, May 14, 1989.

Wertenbaker, Thomas. *Torchbearer of the Revolution.* Princeton, NJ: Princeton University Press, 1940.

ABOUT THE AUTHOR

L.B. Taylor Jr. is a native Virginian. He was born in Lynchburg and has a BS degree in journalism from Florida State University. He wrote about America's space programs for sixteen years—for NASA and aerospace contractors—before moving to Williamsburg, Virginia, in 1974 to work as public affairs director for BASF Corporation. He retired in 1993. Taylor is the author of more than three hundred national magazine articles and forty-five nonfiction books. His research for the book *Haunted Houses*, published by Simon and Schuster in 1983, stimulated his interest in area psychic phenomena and led to the publication of twenty-three books on Virginia ghosts. In 2007, he was presented the Lifetime Achievement Award by the Virginia Writers' Club.

Photo courtesy of Michael Westfall.

Visit us at

www.historypress.net